The Unofficial X-Files Companion

VOLUME III

The Unofficial X-Files Companion

VOLUME III

THE ALL NEW X-PHILE'S GUIDE TO EVEN MORE CONSPIRACIES, MYSTERIES, AND STRANGE EVENTS BEHIND THE SERIES

N. E. Genge

MACMILLAN

As always, this is for my family. I'm so very lucky to have you all.

First published 1997 by Macmillan

an imprint of Macmillan Publishers Ltd
25 Eccleston Place, London SW1W 9NF
and Basingstoke

Associated companies throughout the world

ISBN 0 333 72119 5

1 3 5 7 9 8 6 4 2

A CIP catalogue record for this book is available from
the British Library.

Text design by Mike Wright

Printed and bound in Great Britain by
The Bath Press, Bath

CONTENTS

ACKNOWLEDGMENTS

Writing the acknowledgments for a book like this is probably the scariest part of the whole process. So many wonderful people help bring projects like this together that I'm always afraid I'll forget someone! And, this year, the list is even longer than usual.

Most of the professionals who were kind enough to share office space with me, invite me to their meetings and conferences, introduce me to their patients, colleagues and supervisors, have all been prominently mentioned in the sections devoted to their specialities, but I'd like to take this opportunity to thank you again for sharing your worlds with me. The generosity and honesty with which you responded to my constant questions, the time you took from your busy schedules, and your patience in explaining the more subtle points of your disciplines still amaze me. I imagine I could remain your student for a lifetime and still have more to learn. My sincere thanks.

For odd notes and stacks of books, for introductions to the more unusual collections out there, and for helping ensure I got everything back where it belonged on time, the staff of the Queen Elizabeth II Library of Memorial University (St. John's), the medical library at the Health Science Center (St. John's), the Museum of Medical Oddities (Hachensack), and the Raymond J. Condon Memorial Library and Resource Center (Labrador City), with special thanks to Alexandra Hartmann, Sandra McDonald, Kelsie Wood, Grant Dix, Beth Woodman, and Patricia Ho.

For sharing bandwidth and insights, and for putting up with my periodic disappearances, the Covert Group – you know who you are.

For their continuing assistance in separating fact and fiction, the great people on the Public Relations staff at the Federal Bureau of Investigations – and the colleagues who indulged their requests for yet more information. Specifically, my thanks to Ray, Paul, Harold, Jim and Elaine, who not only answer all my questions with patience and humor, but who can also be counted on to provide hot coffee and homemade Danish (thanks, Paul!) to writers who forget to eat.

For bringing calm and order to the chaos I rather hopefully call my office, for sharing my enthusiasm, for putting up with a schedule that doesn't even attempt to be "normal," and for dozens of other things that have little to do with work, but a whole lot to do with being a terrific person, John W. Sainsbury.

For laughter and hugs, good business advice, and even more things that have nothing to do with work, my agent and friend, Ling Lucas. Thank you.

For helping keep Ling sane enough and organized enough to do all those nice things she does, Ellen van Wees.

For making it a pleasure for a writer in Canada to do business "across the big Pond," and for his understanding and patience, my editor Richard Milner and his colleagues.

And, for gentle humor, compassion, a seemingly unending willingness to listen to disjoint sections in the middle of the night, and for his unflinching support, my husband, Peter.

PHOTOGRAPHIC ACKNOWLEDGMENTS

INTRODUCTION

As *The UnOfficial X-Files Companion III* is tucked in its little box and sent off to the publishers, the cast and crew of *The X-Files*, in a considerably expanded form, are about to start filming their first full-length feature film and fans can't help wondering if we're about to watch the launch of a *Star Trek* styled production schedule with a major film every two years, maybe even a "next genera-tion" of paranormal investigators, or a spin-off series starring The Lone Gunmen in a quest to infiltrate key targets of the military-industrial complex – or the nearest cheese steak shop/adult news stand, whichever is closest.

OK, so maybe the public isn't quite ready for industrial spies on skates, but, it's been an inter-esting year for X-Philes.

First there was the dreaded move to Sunday nights, at least in the US, a schedule change that many American fans predicted would cost the program a large proportion of its viewers – especially if those viewers thought giving the Friday night slot to *Millennium* just to "co-opt" *The X-Files'* fan base was a tad too obvious a marketing ploy. No one need have worried. They moved. *The X-Files'* rating jumped up even higher. *Millennium*, after a settling-in period, found its own niche, its own fans, and it too started climbing higher in the ratings. Though fans had wondered about the wisdom of splitting 10-13s attention between two such technically demanding shows, wondered if

such a division of labor might not produce two watered-down products, neither of which would make the grade, that didn't seem to happen either. Some odd "coincidences" did, of course, pop up from time to time: for example, when the early episodes of both shows featured a sty full of pigs, or when both shows took their leading men up the side of some pretty spectacular snow-covered mountains late in the season, or when *The X-Files* episodes like "Home" were suddenly suffused with the brilliant yellows and blues asso-ciated with The Yellow House scenes instead of the more usual grays and browns, a few jokes about "recycling" and "budgeting" did make the rounds. No one was joking, however, when the words "sexual harassment," "lawsuit" and *X-Files* were used in a single headline in a legitimate industry publication.

The one thing that doesn't seem to have anyone talking is the supposed "death" of Agent Mulder on the couch/bed of his apartment. Perhaps the "boxcar" scenario burnt out fans' Angst-reactors, or perhaps X-Philes are counting up the years rumored to be left in various actors' contracts, or just recognizing that Fox is highly unlikely to let one of its most successful shows to date commit suicide by killing off its leads.

The rumor last year, that both Anderson and Duchovny were looking for time away from the program, the opportunity to work on some of the numerous projects being offered to them, proved true. With some skillful scripting, wonderful episodes like "Memento Mori" and "Musings of a Cigarette-Smoking Man" gave the actors some space from their daily grind while continuing to provide viewers with captivating hours of television. Darin Morgan did indeed leave the writing stable, though you can see him "in the flesh" in "Small Potatoes."

Brother Glen and his writing partner Jim Wong returned between projects to script the sort of shows that had fans loving – or hating – them within minutes of the opening credits, and the sort of shows that stick in the mind long after the last fade out.

The regulars continued to kink the mythology's tail, providing not just one alternate-possibility - for - what - may - have - happened - to - Samantha storyline, but three! While it's true you do need a scorecard to keep up with all the players and theories, not to mention timelines, that have become part of the ongoing X-Filean mythos, episodes like "Paper Hearts" are certainly worth the extra effort. The equally intriguing series of events that began when Gillian Anderson's pregnancy resulted in Dana Scully's abduction finally fulfilled its potential this season, and while it has yet to run its course the connection between the Dynamic Duo, the way their separate searches have joined in a single, smooth storyline, has made for some emotionally satisfying viewing.

As the series moves on to its fifth season, a season that will likely start late to accommodate the filming of the loosely titled "The X-Files: Blackwood", fans know they'll have not only another season of UFOs and MOWs, but a film to look forward to during the next long summer.

CODE NAME:

"Talitha Cumi/ Herrenvolk"

Case: XF-4X01-10-04-96

In Universal's "Lionheart."

CASE SUMMARY

Mulder's attempts to unite Jeremiah Smith, an apparent modern miracle worker, with his dying mother seem doomed when the Bounty Hunter returns from the dead to track them through two countries. When, mere steps ahead of this persistent killer, Mulder discovers a remote farm being worked by a multitude of girls identical to his abducted sister, even his fervent loyalties and long-held priorities become muddled.

CASE HISTORY
Meet: Brian Thompson

Though Brian Thompson is nothing like his *X-Filean* alter ego, the actor and the program do have something in common. Just as *The X-Files* hides its agenda beneath several layers of possibility, Brian Thompson carefully disguised his own hidden agenda, to become an actor, while pursuing a business management degree and tossing footballs at Central Washington University. The man who would send chills up and down the spines of millions of X-Philes was a self-described "closet actor."

How did someone from small-town Washington State get bitten by the acting bug?

"I went to college to play football, I had a scholarship to study the piano . . . My father wanted me to major in business, which I ended up doing, but I played Boris the Russian ballet instructor in *You Can't Take It With You* my spring quarter of my senior year in high school and received the 'Best Supporting Actor of the Year' in my high school for that one shot in a play! . . . It was, absolutely, the most satisfying experience of my entire scholastic career! Beyond the sports! As soon as I got an opportunity to audition for plays in college, I did.

"I didn't study acting formally there though [at Central Washington University], I was kind of a closet drama student. I read every book that the library had on acting and drama. I studied that with my heart where I studied business with my . . . whatever. The business study was by rote, the drama study was, honestly, like an act of freedom.

"And faced with going to work when I got out of college the fall of my senior year or . . . trying something different, I chose the trying something different.

"I had also had some nice successes at that college. I'd auditioned for a well-known summer theater in Colorado and been the only person at the school offered a job, and I had been given their 'Best Actor' award.

"Secretly, there were two books that I had really liked, *Acting Power* and *Acting Professionally*, written by Robert Cohen. These books were in the library, and they weren't advertisements for his school, but it just said in the back, in his bio, that he's a professor of drama at University of California at Irvine.

"So I auditioned for a bunch of acting schools, I secretly wrote away to all these schools – didn't tell anyone! I didn't tell my parents, I didn't tell my friends, I didn't tell anyone!

"I probably was fearful of their . . . shock. No, I just didn't think anyone was going to say, 'Hey, Brian, that's a great idea!' so . . . I didn't tell anyone."

And how did your interest come out?

"I finally had to tell people because the schools wanted letters of recommendation. Then I went to the Drama Department and asked for the letters of recommendation and, of course, then they said, 'Hey, Brian, there'd be a lot of community theaters that would be happy to have you in their troupe.' I said, 'Sorry, I got to try this with a little more . . .'"

A little more focus?

"Yeah, focus. And, I didn't feel that I was ready to go to . . . I mean, the thought of going to LA or New York was just too intimidating! So, I wanted to go to school. I somehow have been a person who has needed 'permission' to do something. I always sort of wanted to get an education. I always wanted to be taught the right technique for a sport before trying it. So I auditioned, and I got almost a full scholarship to go to UCI. I also got to teach acting there for three years while we were going to school. If you teach something, you learn it much better yourself."

Trivia Buster

1

THESE ARE THE EASY ONES! TAKE A SINGLE POINT FOR EACH CORRECT ANSWER.

1. What replaced "The Truth Is Out There" in this episode's credits?

2. Through which Canadian province did Jeremiah lead Mulder?

3. How many entries, roughly, did Pendrell figure were in the files of the Jeremiah Smiths?

4. To what bizarre hideout does "Samantha" lead Mulder?

5. What does X scrawl on the floor in blood?

THESE WILL MAKE YOU THINK, SO GIVE YOURSELF TWO POINTS FOR A CORRECT RESPONSE.

6. For what company did the ill-fated linesman work?

7. What did the "SEP" sections of the computer entries stand for?

8. What was the number of Mrs. Mulder's hospital room?

9. What do Pendrell and Scully give up in the name of scientific investigation?

10. To what did Skinner compare Scully's "evidence"?

1

Answers

KEEP TRACK OF YOUR TOTAL SCORE. SEE WHERE YOU'D END UP IN THE X-FILEAN WORLD OF HIERARCHIES, SHADOW GOVERNMENTS, AND CONSPIRACIES.

ONE POINTERS:

1. "Everything Dies"

2. Alberta.

3. A billion.

4. An apiary.

5. SRSG.

TWO POINTERS:

6. Telus.

7. Smallpox Eradication Program.

8. 128.

9. Tissue for a biopsy from their smallpox vaccines.

10. Images from the Hubble telescope.

YOUR SCORE _____

So, you'd made the shift to drama, what did you think of formal drama studies?

"Once at UCI, things just went really well. At the end of the first year, I was the only actor who was selected to go to the Colorado Shakespeare Festival, even though all of us had auditioned. There was a three-year program and all three years are auditioned and I'd never even done Shakespeare! And here I was allowed to go to this prestigious festival.

"And then, the following year, I started auditioning for equity theaters around LA and got a job doing *Bittersweet* with Shirley Jones and did the King in *The King and I* out at Riverside Civic Light Opera. I also started auditioning out in Hollywood. I got an agent and I got this job at Universal Studios Tour, doing the Conan Show."

Oh, I remember that! Twelve minutes, four times a day?

"Yes, a little eighteen-minute play. My transition from school to the professional world was seamless."

Much gentler than many actors', wasn't it?

"My last year in school, I kept the job at Universal Studios Tour. I was on the MCA stock investment plan, had full health coverage, had a pension plan."

An actor with a pension plan? I love it! Maybe some of that business degree rubbed off?

"Well, the only thing that did is that when people said, 'Acting is a business. If you want to make a living, you have to approach it as a business.' There wasn't any confusion about that sentence. You know, that's marketing, that's selling yourself to as many markets as you can, good art work, good printwork. I, without a doubt, had the best picture and résumé of all the actors that were graduating that year. It was more polished. I had access to the mainframe computers – back then PCs were just coming out, in '84 – so I was able to use all the facilities over in the Computer Department and I had nice résumés. Presentation. Presentation."

And the other thing, of course, is location. Location. Location. Location. And, by this time, you'd made that gradual move, hadn't you, from your small town of Ellensburg, WA, to a larger centre when you went to Central Washington University, and an even larger one in Irvine, from which you could dabble in Los Angeles?

"Exactly, and the school was close to LA and, well [*drawls*] I knew they made movies up thar. Up north of the school. But, you know, I never thought I would be in films and television really, until, it was the end of my second year at Irvine, I had auditioned for five summer theaters and been offered a job at all of them. And I'd also been cast fifth of five for that job in the Conan show, at the Tour, which meant that I wouldn't have a job for the summer, yet here I had a job, with some great parts, up at PCPA Theater Fest in Solvang, Santa Maria, and that theater gets reviewed by, like, the *LA Times*, it gets reviewed by the big San Francisco papers. It's probably the best summer stock on the entire west coast. And I had a job there! But I also had a shot at a job at Universal Studios! The night before I was supposed to leave for Solvang, I spoke with another actor, Ron Batham, at South Coast Repertory Theater, who had been an equity actor all his life. In fact, I'd gone that night to see him in *Henry IV, Part Two*. I presented to him my predicament and he just said, 'Well, what do you want to do? Look at it, do you want to be my age, forty, with roommates, not really being able to afford kids, bouncing around, doing that, but having played some really great parts in equity theaters? If you want to do that, go to PCPA. Or do you want to take a shot at being in films and television? If you want to do that, hey, you should probably keep your job at Universal Studios.' And that was the moment! That night, I realized, Hey, I really would like to be in a film! And, before that, I'd never even thought that!"

A rather rapid transition, then?

"Yeah, it was a deciding moment. And, the next day, at the rehearsal for the Conan show, one of the guys in front of me

X BLOOPER! The bloopers started early in season four, and early in this episode – just check out the opening scene with its five identical boys! The special effects, that have been praised so deservedly in this and other episodes, didn't quite extend to the little details – like two distinct sets of shadows! Maybe it makes up for the fact that the bright red pylon standing next to the boys casts no shadow at all.

In "Commando Squad"

blew his knee out! And about three days later, another guy just got scared. We had to do a eighteen-foot-high fall through a ring of fire and he kind of broke out in hives when he actually got up there to fall the first time. He wouldn't do it. So that, all together, moved me right up to third spot, and I had a job for the whole summer. Then, at the end of the summer, when they cut it down to just two cast-members, I was chosen to be one of the two that were to stay on. I got to do that job every Friday, Saturday and Sunday for my last year in school. By the end of that summer, I'd gotten an agent, I'd started going to auditions.

"The first audition I went to was for the movie *Vision Quest*, at Warner Brothers. And the next day they had me on a plane and flew me back to Washington State, sort of back to the beginning, up to Spokane, to meet the director because they thought I was really quite right for the part of one of the wrestlers. I didn't get the job, but that was my first audition ever for Hollywood."

With a history like that, do you believe in fate?

"Well, sometimes. If you can picture the future working out in your mind, it's kind of an active fantasy that stays with you. Then I think you can have that direction. Fate, to me, should apply to world leaders, great inventors, not really to actors."

What would you love to do?

"The generic answer to that question is that I just like to be associated with good projects, but I like to be involved in the telling of great tales that repeat and eviscerate the universal human truths. That's why I became an actor, to stand there, feet anchored on the ground, and speak the best lines ever written, to speak the words that talk about humanity. That's some of the best literature ever made!"

What about your future?

"I would honestly say I like the idea of hacking out new territory. I mean, I have lots of friends who say, 'I'd love to play

In *X-Files* episode
"Kindred: The Embrace"

Hamlet. I want to play Macbeth. I want to play whoever.' I don't. I would do that, I could be very excited by it, I probably will do that, but, when we talk about the active fantasy we have for our futures, concretely, I'd like to approach them to redo Sheriff Cody as a half-hour comedy and see how a Zen-Buddist sheriff would handle himself. It was never developed as an idea. I think I'm going to pitch that. There's also two companies who are actively searching for scripts for me. I'd never realized how hard it was to find good scripts, it's been opening my eyes a bit."

As Sheriff Cody in Fox's
TV series "Key West"

Your fantasy project?

"There's this French windsurfer, incredible story, and I've been really trying to figure out how Hollywood could do a windsurfing story, but you'd really need a windsurfer, or a sailor, to write this story. I hear all this dialogue for this character in my head. He was like the Evil Knevel of windsurfing, he crossed the Sahara on a big windsurfing/skateboard with huge balloon tires! He sailed across the Baltic Sea to Russia, had all his equipment confiscated, then charmed them all so much that they let him come back! He disappeared, sailing, in warm waters, in Communist waters, trying to cross the Taiwan Strait. It's theorized that he may just have been picked up by the Chinese government and locked away. They never found any trace of him and, well, everything that he had floats! It excites me a great deal to play someone who's a real person."

(Interviewer's note: Brian Thompson has also written two articles about his favourite sport for *American Windsurfing*. Wonder if there's some hitherto unknown connection between boards and *The X-Files*?)

How did you come to audition for *The X-Files*?

"It was 100 percent agency organized."

Had you seen *The X-Files*?

"No. I had no idea what the show was. I'd been in Europe basically from June to December of 1994 and it was a December interview. I'd only been back a few days and I went in and met

X If you've ever wondered how many takes go into a scene of *The X-Files*, you might want to check out the number of times Pendrell's tie moves up and down during his discussion with Scully of smallpox and cowpox.

X Though David Duchovny has given up a lot for his craft, even he's not about to spend take after take sharing scenes with bees. The "apiary" residents seen on screen were a combination of real bees and their computer-generated kin.

Chris Carter and the director of the episode, Rob Bowman, who'd directed a lot of the episodes. Rob had directed the first *Star Trek* episode that I'd been in, "A Matter of Honor" – one of the benchmark TNG episodes – so I knew Rob was a great director and my agents told me the show was great, so, on that basis, I decided to do it. I didn't know anything about it really. I went up to Canada, up to BC, and promptly got into a huge fight over my hair with the producers! I'm telling you, it was . . . They wanted me to cut my hair. At the time, it was shoulder-length, the length it was in *Dragonheart*, and I was up for a couple of feature films where they wanted my hair left longer

The Heroes of Desert Storm (1992) – Specialist Alston

Revolver (1992) – Ken

"Disney Presents The 100 Lives of Black Jack Savage" (1991)
   – Black Jack Savage

"The Whereabouts of Jenny" (1991) – Mick

"21 Jump Street" (1987) – Captain Adam Fuller

"Dreams of Gold: The Mel Fisher Story" (1986) – Mo

House (1986) – Cop #4

"The Equalizer" (1985) – Lt. Burnett

Better Off Dead (1985) – Tree Trimmer

"International Airport" (1985) – Frazier

Missing in Action 2: The Beginning (1985) – Nester

Rambo: First Blood Part II (1985) – Lifer

"Triplecross" (1985) – Kyle Banks

Twilight Zone: The Movie (1983) – Bar Patron

The Blues Brothers (1980) –Trooper Mount

Big Apple Birthday (1978) – More Fairy Tale Folk

In addition, he's guested on over a dozen television series including *Models Inc., Sister, Sister, Diagnosis Murder, Hangin' with Mr.
Cooper, Booker, Wiseguy, SeaQuest DSV, Stingray, MacGyver, L.A.
Law, Remington Steele, Hunter, Hill Street Blues* and even a couple
episodes of *Dallas*.

"Is this any way to treat the man
who is dangling a miracle in front
of you?"

X Filming for the
"Herrenvolk" episode ran
longer than almost any
other episode.

X For four seasons,
X-Philes have been
calling Mrs. Mulder just that
– Mrs. Mulder. According to
actress Rebecca Toolan, who
plays the slowly recovering
maternal influence in Fox
Mulder's life, the hospital
band worn in both "Talitha
Cumi" and "Herrenvolk"
identified her as Elizabeth
Mulder.

so, I had told them, 'Yes, you can cut it, but I want it left long
on top and we can just go ahead and slick it down and you can
cut it short in the back.' And that's all that was said. Basically,
'Will he cut his hair?' and 'Yes.' Well, I get up there and they
wanted me to have a crew cut. No one had said crew cut. And
it turned into this big, huge fight. Chris Carter was calling my
agents at home and my agent were calling me on my cellular
phone in the make-up trailer and it was this big ugly Thing.
Everyone hated me all of a sudden because I wouldn't have a
crew cut, but no one had said anything about a crew cut to me
and I certainly didn't want to get cut out of my shot at these

Mulder must have trouble keeping track of all his "sisters." After having the adult version visit earlier last year, he tracked down the stuck-in-time version in the season premiere.

other feature films – and the military thing was not the right look for these other roles.

"Anyway, that Thing eventually calmed down, but I could tell the producers were thinking I was Mr. Trouble-Maker. I went home that weekend, got to the airport on Sunday evening and the girl at the airport says, 'Hey, congratulations!' I just look at her and say, 'For what?' and she says, 'Your show. It won "Best Dramatic Series" at the Golden Globes!' It was that week. I just went, to myself, 'Wha'?' Wow! I had no idea the show was that good. I still hadn't seen an episode yet! So, anyway, I went up to Canada with kind of a change of heart. I'd stepped into something really special and just had no time to think about it. Sometimes, you know, you work and you work and you work and you finally get to a place and when you get there, you know the story, but this whole thing just enveloped around me and it always improved. You know, the character kept developing, becoming more dimensional, and it's kind of like a little family up there now and I feel very lucky that the character I play got involved in the mythology. That was a stroke of luck also."

When you started doing this role, basically, how did they describe this character to you?

"Well, it was minimal, really minimal. Basically, that there was this illegal colonization of clones and that I am an alien. They called me the Alien Bounty Hunter originally. David [Duchovny] called me the Alien Booty Hunter. And that these clones all had to be terminated and I was the man for the job. They only had the first script at that point, and they'd said that, in the second half he's got a lot more to do in the second script, he's got a lot more dialogue and yadda-yadda."

That didn't materialize?

"No, that became a fight also because the second script came out and there's nothing! It's the same as the first, wandering around killing people and says about three lines! So, I go to the producer and say, 'Look, I want to go home. You think I'm a jerk, but just morph me into somebody else and I'll go home. This isn't what I signed on for, it isn't what I wanted.'

"So, then, the scene in the submarine, with David, where he learns about his sister, got written. It wasn't in there in the beginning, it was written because I told them I wanted to morph and go home! I don't want to just walk around. I don't want to play an automaton. Who wants to be an automaton? Why?

"Then they took the character, after that, in the next couple of episodes, and took him way beyond that and had him perform this miracle and save Mulder's mother at the end of the last show! ["Talitha Cumi"] And that was entirely their own doing."

Do they give you any idea of where the character is going to go? Or do they just deliver the script and you adjust each time around?

"Well, at this point the character can go anywhere. He could be in a coffee shop having a wonderful conversation with some beautiful woman. He could be working in a nursery. Who knows? The sky's the limit."

Have they written him into the movie?

"No. I don't think this is going to be a mythology episode."

If you could nudge the writers in a particular direction for your character, what would you like to see?

"I love the mystical stuff, but at the same time I like that tie to a person who has a very perfunctory, nasty job to do. I would like them to expose a few more of the secrets of why he's doing this or who he's working for, but, honestly, I don't allow myself to even speculate about where they'll take him next."

Filmography: Brian Thompson
Mortal Kombat: Annihilation (1997) – Shao Kahn
"Babylon 5" [Racing Mars] (1997) – Smuggler
"Buffy the Vampire Slayer" [Premiere] (1997) – Luke

X Chris Carter's fascination with unusual titles certainly continued from the get-go in season four. "Herrenvolk" translates to "master race," "folk of the lords," or "supreme beings." Its close connotations with Nazism and the terror inflicted by those who last claimed the title give "herrenvolk" a lingering aura of dark schemes, scientific depravity and covert government approval.

CASE CREDITS

WRITTEN BY: Chris Carter
DIRECTED BY: R.W. Goodwin
ORIGINAL PRODUCTION
    NUMBER: 4X01
ORIGINAL US AIR DATE: 10/04/96

GUEST CAST

JEREMIAH SMITH
    Roy Thinnes
ASSISTANT DIRECTOR WALTER
S. SKINNER
    Mitch Pileggi
AGENT PENDRELL
    Brendan Beiser
MRS. MULDER
    Rebecca Toolan
THE CIGARETTE-SMOKING MAN
    William B. Davis
X
    Steven Williams
ALIEN BOUNTY HUNTER
    Brian Thompson
THE ELDER
    Don Williams
GREY-HAIRED MAN
    Morris Panych
THE REPAIRMAN
    Garvin Cross

DEATH TOLL

1 MAN: stung to death

"Kindred: The Embraced" (1996) – Eddie Fiori
"Deep Space Nine" (1996) – Jem'Haedar Second in Command
Dragonheart (1996) – Brock
"Hercules: The Legendary Journeys" [Siege At Naxos] (1995)
    – Goth the Barbarian
Star Trek: Generations (1994) – Klingon Helm
"Key West" (1993) – Sheriff Cody Jeremiah Jefferson
Doctor Mordrid (1992) – Kabal
The Naked Truth (1992)
Rage and Honor (1992) – Conrad Drago
Hired to Kill (1991) – Frank Ryan
Life Stinks (1991) – Mean Victor
"The Owl" (1991) – Barkeeper
Ted and Venus (1992) – Herb
"After the Shock" (1990) – Tom
Lionheart (1990) – Russel
Fright Night Part II (1989) – Bocworth
In the Cold of the Night (1989) – Phil
Miracle Mile (1989) – Power Lifter
Moon 44 (1989) – Jake O'Neal
Nightwish (1989)
"The Next Generation" [A Matter of Honor] (1987) – Klag
"Favorite Son" (1988) – Peterson
Alien Nation (1988) – Trent Porter
Pass the Ammo (1988) – Kenny Hamilton
"Werewolf" (1987)
Catch the Heat (1987) – Danny Boy
Commando Squad (1987)
You Talkin' to Me? (1987) – James
Cobra (1986) – Night Slasher
Three Amigos! (1986) – German's Other Friend
"Moonlighting" (1985) – Simon's Man
"Fatal Vision" (1984) – Lieutenant Harrison
Terminator (1984) – Punk
Bush Christmas (1983) – Bookmaker
"Knight Rider" [Sky Knight] (1985) – Kurt

CODE NAME:

"Unruhe"

CASE SUMMARY

A trail of disturbing photos – which Mulder claims are the psychic imprints of a demented man's mind – is the only tangible clue in a series of kidnappings. Back-alley lobotomies, outdated pharmaceuticals, and the murmuring of the kidnapper's first victim provide Scully with less supernatural, if more perplexing, clues to the killer's identity. Ironically, she soon finds herself hoping Mulder's theory proves more substantial than she'd originally believed – how else will he locate her when she becomes victim number three?

CASE HISTORY
Pictures worth a thousand words?

For long-time viewers of *The X-Files*, "Unruhe" was like a trip down memory lane. Here, gathered in one episode, were all the classic X-Filean elements which had drawn viewers away from other, more heavily hyped, programs and into *The X-Files* right from the very beginning! It was a veritable checklist for "How To Produce An Episode Of *The X-Files*." Everything from "Have Scully Lift Eyebrow 14 Times" to "Just A Touch Of Almost Personal Conversation" to the all-important "Give 'Em Something To Argue About!"

Sure viewers love the close, claustrophobic atmosphere of the "mythology" episodes, the cases that supposedly pull us just a tad closer to finding Samantha and figuring out the grand scheme of conspiracies. Who wouldn't? But, every now and then, X-Philes want to see something, anything, even if it is just a one-off episode – with a villain who'll never see the light of day again in courtroom, psychiatric hospital or laboratory – *resolved*. Like addicts, X-Philes crave the five or six episodes a season that revolve around Mulder making The Incredible Claim, Scully riposting with The Rational Response, and the two of them sniping at one another for the remainder of the episode until whoever, or whatever, they're tracking eventually

EYEWITNESS STATEMENT

"She's been given what's called a transorbital lobotomy. It used to be known as an 'icepick' lobotomy. It involves inserting a leucotome through the eye socket."
Special Agent Dana Scully

gets killed, kills her-him-itself, or disappears in a manner designed to suggest the possibility of a sequel episode. So, it's no real surprise that just such an episode would be chosen for airing when the program made its big move to Sunday nights. If the "classic" structure could keep people home on a Friday night, then why couldn't lightning strike twice on Sunday?

And what better topic for a classic episode than something like "thoughtography"? A more perfect bone to be picked over in the great Incredible Claim vs. Rational Response debate would be tough to find. It's kept parapsychologists, physicists, psychologists, medical doctors and magicians occupied for nearly half a century. Surely it could keep Scully and Mulder occupied for 45 minutes!

Though "thoughtography," also called "psychic photography" has only been around since the 60s, the "skotography" Mulder mentions does indeed go back to the very beginnings of modern image collection. Skotographs, photos which their owners claim include incredible images that the photographer didn't see when taking the photo, or photographs purporting to be deliberate attempts to capture supernatural phenomena, have surfaced fairly consistently from the time the first Daguerreotypist left his thumb dangling until the present. In fact, one form of skotography has actually been on the rise in the past few years!

While taking pictures of ghostly apparitions has sort of fallen off as a hobby since technology progressed to the point when it can easily distinguish between a flash-light illuminated piece of cheesecloth and a wandering spirit, "miracle" photographs are popping up almost every day. In Brazil, an amateur shutterbug was shocked to discover Jesus Christ himself leering up at him from his tray of developing solution as the clouds in one of his pictures suddenly resolved into an image he'd never even noticed while taking the landscape shots he'd hoped to turn into postcards. Instead, he printed the images

Trivia Buster

2

THESE ARE THE EASY ONES! TAKE A SINGLE POINT FOR EACH CORRECT ANSWER.

1. For what unconnected crime was Mary LaFante being investigated?

2. How were the male victims killed?

3. What odd apparatus is Gerry Schnauz wearing when Scully meets him?

4. What was Gerald Schnauz Sr.'s profession?

5. What was the date on the druggist's film supply?

THESE WILL MAKE YOU THINK, SO GIVE YOURSELF TWO POINTS FOR A CORRECT RESPONSE.

6. At what pharmacy did Mary LeFante have her picture taken?

7. What pharmaceutical substances were found in Mary LeFante?

8. Scully finds identical signs at two crime scenes. What was the company?

9. What did Gerry Schnauz believe lived in his head?

10. What were both Alice and Mary wearing when they were found?

▶

Trivia Buster

2

Answers

KEEP TRACK OF YOUR TOTAL SCORE. SEE WHERE YOU'D END UP IN THE X-FILEAN WORLD OF HIERARCHIES, SHADOW GOVERNMENTS, AND CONSPIRACIES.

ONE POINTERS:

1. Tampering with federal mail, credit card theft, and forgery.

2. The insertion of some sharp object through the ear into the brain.

3. Plasterer's slits.

4. He was a dentist.

5. 4/94.

TWO POINTERS:

6. Kelso's Drugs.

7. "Twilight Sleep," a dental anaesthetic made of morphine and scopolamine.

8. Iskendanian Construction– Renovation.

9. The Howlers.

10. A nightgown.

YOUR SCORE _____

on cheaper paper, sold them in front of a church where he claimed they were proof of God's existence in the modern world, and pocketed, according to the church's best estimates, the equivalent of 7,500 American dollars. The church eventually asked to have him removed from the front of their property as he was "a public nuisance that interfered with the normal trade of the church."

Not all skotographs, however, are of tree mould that mysteriously forms itself into images of the Virgin Mary, or piles of refuse at a landfill site that, if viewed just so, might, by those with good imaginations, resemble the final scene from your child's Christmas play, complete with shepherds. Most skotographs are even *more* amorphous. In December of 1994, Dana Plack of Detroit took home her latest batch of photographs and was busily grinning over the captured antics of the family's two-year-old daughter when one photo literally left her speechless. Wordlessly handing over the picture to her husband, she pointed to what appeared to be a shadowy Death, complete with the billowing robes and sickle, leaning over the toddler. Both parents were shaken and asked a photographer friend to see what he made of the print. Their relief when he duplicated the picture with the assistance of a conveniently placed plant hanger and the afternoon sunlight streaming through an equally convenient window was considerable.

No one, however, was able to do the same for Gordon and Lydia Totten of Toronto when their holiday pictures unexpectedly revealed a ghostly aura surrounding Lydia's mother, though several experts did try. The confounding factors in this case were highly technical. While not every picture on the roll included Lydia's mother, not one picture of her was without the "aura." The affected pictures didn't follow a pattern as might be found if the film had been accidentally exposed. The camera, examined by the manufacturer on two separate occasions, functioned perfectly under stringent test conditions. Still, despite the lack of evidence to support any sort of theory, several photographers suggest there might have been a problem with the film before it was loaded into the camera. The incident will likely retain its mystery, at least for the Totten family, if only because the questioned photos turned out to be the last taken of the 83-year-old woman who died of natural causes within the week.

Like skotography, "thought" photography's perceived validity, or lack thereof, often depends on the ability to judge the technical components of the setup, the controls placed on experimental settings, the interpretation of the images, if any, collected, and the procedure undertaken by the thoughtographer. In other words, a situation more perfectly designed for integration into an *X-Files* episode would be hard to find. Scully's healthy scepticism for photos taken outside a controlled environment, with outdated and overheated film, accurately reflects the general feeling within the limited scientific world actually studying thoughtographs. Mulder's "open-minded" stance, however, also turns up among researchers – even those with considerably less detailed pictures that the ones Mulder discovered.

Ted Serios, the bellhop Mulder mentions to Scully, was probably the first thoughtographer to gain widespread notoriety. Born in 1920, Serios was the prima donna study subject of Dr. Jule Eisenbud and a group of parapsychologists who spent several years testing his ability. Serios's early images were detailed and, even to a sceptical interpreter, likely to bear some resemblance to whatever image he claimed he intended to record. Some images, of recognizable locations and famous people, were unquestionable, if blurry or distorted. Later images became less and less detailed, some no more than blobs which Ted Serios dubbed "blackies" and "whities." In 1967, Eisenbud published a book, *The World of Ted Serios*, which

X Even a cursory study of X-Filean episode titles introduces the viewer to several foreign languages, though German seemed to enjoy a certain prominence with titles like "Die Hand Die Verletzt" and "Herrenvolk" topping out the list before this episode, "Unruhe," came along. Among the many English-language synonyms for "unruhe" are "concern," "disquietude," "fidget," "fidgetiness," "inquietude," "restiveness," "trouble," "unease," "uneasiness," "unrest," and, in combination and phrases, like "unruhe stiften," "to riot," and "to disturb the peace."

included dozens of photographs. Ironically, it was these photographs which themselves would later be considered proof that Ted Serios had been creating his pictures not with his mind, but with a palm-able hand-held device capable of altering the film inside the camera casing. Though Eisenbud

NOTEBOOK

Guest Filmography: Pruitt Taylor Vince

Despite an intriguing filmography, with some challenging roles to his credit, Pruitt Vince may well be best remembered by X-Philes as the man who dared injury to Dana Scully's dainty foot!

"Night Sins" (1997) – Olie Swain

Beautiful Girls (1996) – Stanley Womack

Heavy (1995) – Victor

Under the Hula Moon (1995) – Bob

China Moon (1994) – Daryl Jeeters

City Slickers II: The Legend of Curly's Gold (1994) – Bud

Natural Born Killers (1994) – Kavanaugh

Nobody's Fool (1994) – Rub Squeers

"Highlander" [The Innocent] – Mickey

"'Til Death Us Do Part" (1992) – Michael Brockington

"Dead in the Water" (1991) – Lou Rescetti

JKF (1991) – Lee Bowers

"Sweet Poison" (1991) – Coyle

Come See the Paradise (1990) – Augie Farrell

Jacob's Ladder (1990) – Paul

Wild at Heart (1990) – Buddy

Homer & Eddie (1990) – Cashier

K-9 (1989) – Benny the Mule

"Quantum Leap" [Moments to Live] – Hank Pilcher

Mississippi Burning (1988) – Lester Cowans

continued to support the integrity of the images, hoax-busters like James Randi weakened the evidence considerably by duplicating Serios's images with their own sleight of hand technologies.

Another American thoughtographer supposedly subjected to rigorous study was Stella Lansing of Michigan. Unlike Serios, who specialized in photographic expressions of his psychic talents, Lansing brought a remarkable history to her new skill, thoughtography. Moving furniture, the knocking of poltergeists, and the appearance of ghostly apparitions were familiar events. Her investigator, Dr. Berthold Schwarz, confined his inquiries to the images she produced on Polaroid films, but, despite narrowing the field of research, and spending several years on the problem, never produced anything even approximating an explanation for the phenomena.

Of course, the subjects themselves, the human element, often confound the investigative process even further. Ted Serios, for example, demands he work through a black box he called his "gizmo." Although the box, examined many times, seems perfectly innocuous, its presence in an otherwise controlled experimental setup breeds mistrust and scepticism. Another thoughtographer, Willie Schwanholz, makes studying his "technique" difficult by insisting he bounce the camera off his forehead to create his images. Masuaki Kiyota, who came to prominence during the 70s, felt a strong need to physically handle the film packs before attempting to imprint images. Somehow, it's easier to accept that Maria Prettachia can't perform her violin solos before packed houses without wearing her mother's locket, a well-documented fact, than to accept that these thoughtograph impresarios can't create without their own idiosyncratic aids. Especially in cases like Masuaki Kiyota, coincidentally another of Dr. Jule Eisenbud's proteges, who is reputed to have been caught on film himself – while in the process of hoaxing yet another talent, spoon-bending.

A damsel in distress? Not always. Remember "Deep Throat" and a host of other episodes where *Scully* is the knight in shining armour.

X Although this episode was second in season four's production, it was delayed until *The X-Files* made its American move to Sunday night. The decision to hold it back was based on the belief that this was such a strong stand-alone episode that new viewers wouldn't have to know the show's history to be caught up in the drama. It seems to have worked. Since moving to Sunday nights, ratings have actually managed to increase!

WRITTEN BY: Vince Gilligan
DIRECTED BY: Rob Bowman
ORIGINAL PRODUCTION
    NUMBER: 4X02
ORIGINAL US AIR DATE: 27/10/96

GUEST CAST

SHARON ALEXANDER
    Mary LeFante
THE BOYFRIEND
    Scott Heindl
THE DRUGGIST
    Walter Marsh
THE DOCTOR
    Michele Melland
GERRY SCHNAUZ
    Pruitt Vince
OFFICER TROTT
    William MacDonald
INSPECTOR PUETT
    Ron Chartier
ALICE
    Angela Donahue

DEATH TOLL

2 MEN: 2 dead by "awl" through
    ear into brain
1 WOMAN: lobotomized

Passing off all psychic photography as nothing more than a new game for hoaxers and investigators to play somewhere on the edges of real science, however, would be as scientifically unsound as simply accepting the claims of every kook with a camera. Some psychic photographers, like Ren Hope, an English medium and the first documented case involving the mysterious images some fifty years ago, were studied under incredibly rigorous conditions that might even have satisfied Scully! Hope had no prior contact with the films, didn't physically handle the cameras, and was provided with either verbal descriptions of the images to create, or with ordinary photographs, just moments to commencing the test. While he never achieved results as spectacular as Serios's early efforts, the results were, more importantly from a scientific stand-point, *consistent* from the beginning of the study to the end when the investigators reluctantly admitted they could find no source, other than Hope himself, that could account for the images. James Cornell, Patricia Speck, Ngaio Cleary and Benjamin Dobbs are all thoughtographers who not only provided images on demand, under conditions Serios and others would have described as "trying," but who have never been involved in "performances" for a non-scientific audiences. Neither have they ever garnered a single cent from their activities.

With *respected* scientists and physical technicians lining up on both sides to support or rebut the existence of psychic photography, it was only a matter of time before some writer wove the offbeat argument into an *X-File*. What continues to delight and surprise X-Philes is that Vince Gilligan did just that in the midst of one of the most terrifying episodes of the season!

CODE NAME:

"Home"

Case: XF-4X03-10-11-96

X Through the magnificent efforts of the special effects crews, Karin Konoval, who appeared hale and whole in *Ebbie, Spoils of War, Double, Double, Toil and Trouble,* not to mention *For the Love of My Child: The Anissa Ayala Story* where she convincingly portrayed a dance instructor, appeared as a quad-amputee in "Home"!

EYEWITNESS STATEMENT

"The Peacocks built that farm during the Civil War. It still has no electricity, no running water, no heat. They grow their own food. They raise their own pigs. They breed their own cows . . . They raise and breed their own . . . 'stock,' if you get my meaning."

Sheriff Andy Taylor

CASE SUMMARY

Scully and Mulder find themselves in a modern Mayberry when they investigate the infanticide of a horribly deformed child in a community with a population of less than a city block. Of those, however, just three have caught Mulder's eye. Three brothers whose own unusual physiologies are already ensuring the entire town stays at more than arm's distance.

CASE HISTORY
The Following Program . . .

The "Parental Advisory" flashing across the screen just before "Home" aired should have been enough to warn X-Philes that the upcoming episode would be . . . different. After all, an overgrown parasite, a fat-sucking sexual deviant with a "taste" for his dates as well as Italian poetry, and yet another cannibal who yanked out his victims' livers with his bare hands all made it to the little screen without the dreaded warning.

With *The X-Files*'s usual knack for twisting its audience's perceptions a full hundred-and-eighty degrees from the expected, however, the biggest shocker of the evening turned out to be the utter humanity of not only the victims, but their killers as well.

Though the "inbred community where strange things happen and even the cops are afraid to step in" has certainly been done well many times, "Home" was something of a first for television. The violence, the sharply contrasting settings, and the startling imagery combined for a shocking, but oddly compelling, hour. Even weeks later, after other, equally intriguing episodes intervened, fans would find themselves thinking about "Home." It was a program that got under the skin, leaving something behind to remind viewers of it at the oddest times. Its duality, the separation between brilliantly lit views of small town life and the dark brooding Peacock residence, created a degree of tension unusual even in an episode of *The*

X-Files. It was designed to create powerful conflicts in viewers, and it did just that. Despite the violent acts committed, despite the brutish portrayal of the Peacocks, and despite the sympathy viewers felt for the victims, few watching could feel totally at ease in their condemnation of the Peacocks. It was meant to be disturbing on as many levels as the talented cast and crew could make it, and it undoubtedly worked!

For some viewers, however, it wasn't the *content* of the episode that actually disturbed them. It was the Parental Advisory.

Charles Critten of the Canadian Association for Quality Television, a group that has monitored the content of American programs coming across the border for nearly twenty years, is puzzled by the warning. "Of course, the program was startling. It's not every day viewers get to see a child delivered in a kitchen where dirty utensils take the place of surgical equipment. I mean, that's definitely a first, but – and it's a big but – *but* was the scene inherently any more violent than, for example, the unending shootouts found in other programs? I don't think so."

The Christian Coalition for Television Awareness appears to agree with him. "You'd be amazed at the number of children in this country [USA] who spend six or seven hours a day watching people jump in and out of bed with one another, kill one another, throw one another down wells, steal one another's children, and try to make away with one another in the most cold-blooded ways possible. And that's daytime TV!" Peirsa Conden, who has just finished watching "Home" for the third time, shrugs, "It's mostly lighting and sound. Actual on-screen violence is minimal. Even during the double murder at the Sheriff's home, it's not the degree of on-screen violence that's really shocking. We're *told* the man was pulped, we don't *see* it happening. We know the wife is killed, but, likewise, we don't *see* anything. It's the single-mindedness of the assailants

3

THESE ARE THE EASY ONES! TAKE A SINGLE POINT FOR EACH CORRECT ANSWER.

1. Where was the dead baby buried?

2. What room became a makeshift autopsy bay for Scully?

3. What sort of car did the Peacock brothers drive?

4. What was Mulder trying, unsuccessfully, to watch on TV?

5. What sort of livestock did the Peacocks raise?

THESE WILL MAKE YOU THINK, SO GIVE YOURSELF TWO POINTS FOR A CORRECT RESPONSE.

6. What product did Scully jokingly proclaim herself spokesperson for?

7. What kind of sandwich did Mulder eat as a kid on the Vineyard?

8. What was Sheriff Taylor's address?

9. How old were the three Peacock brothers?

10. To whom does Mulder compare Deputy Barney?

Answers

KEEP TRACK OF YOUR TOTAL SCORE. SEE WHERE YOU'D END UP IN THE X-FILEAN WORLD OF HIERARCHIES, SHADOW GOVERNMENTS, AND CONSPIRACIES.

ONE POINTERS:

1. A makeshift ballfield, near home plate.

2. A sink-and-toilet-only washroom in the police station.

3. A Cadillac.

4. A New York Nicks game.

5. Pigs.

TWO POINTERS:

6. The Ab-Roller.

7. Bologna.

8. 3 Sweetgum Lane, Home, Pennsylvania.

9. Edmund Creighton Peacock, 42; George Raymond Peacock, 30; and Sherman Nathaniel Peacock, 26.

10. Charles Bronson.

YOUR SCORE _____

NOTEBOOK

"Where Do You Get Your Ideas?"

Every writer on the planet is inevitably asked two questions: "Have you published anything yet?" immediately followed by "Where do you get your ideas?"

A simple yes-no handles the first one, but most writers blunder about a bit when explaining a process which drags several disparate experiences from the murky depths of the subconscious, tweaks them, and then squeezes them into something completely individual

"Home," however, had more obvious roots.

No one who has ever read *Charles Chaplin: My Autobiography* (reprint, Plume, 1993), which spans the silent film comic's life, could possibly forget young Chaplin's meeting with Gilbert, a grotesquely dwarfed and deformed real-life character who lurked beneath the furniture in one of the many boarding houses where Chaplin stayed during his touring years. Gilbert, having been evicted from his room to make space for Chaplin, the paying guest, remained hidden until his family callously induced him to come out and do tricks for the visitors. How could a Chaplin fan like Glen Morgan, with the opportunity to write edgy scripts for a hot television program already famous for its creative imagery, be expected *not* to weave such bizarre tidbits into his work!

Another inspiration, even above and beyond the slobbish family who once lived in the Morgans' neighbourhood and had their name bestowed on the inbred Peacocks, was a startling 1992 documentary, *Brother's Keeper*, by Joe Berlinger and Bruce Sinofsky, which delved into the lives of the four Ward Brothers who lived on the outskirts of Munnville, New York. Like the Peacocks, the Wards lived in slovenly conditions, ostracized by a community content enough to simply ignore them – until one brother is accused of murdering another. Though Delbert Ward reputedly confessed readily enough to savagely killing brother William, *Brother's Keeper* presents compelling evidence that not only was Delbert mentally incapable of giving an informed consent to the waiving of all his constitutional rights, but that his confession was artfully staged by big city cops who wanted closure over justice. Almost as shocking as the conditions under which the men lived, however, was the surprising fervour Delbert's arrest stirred up. Suddenly, and with the same thoroughness with which they'd previously ignored the brothers, the town closed ranks around them, defending Delbert and casting pointed aspersions at the "outsiders."

Guest Filmography: Tucker Smallwood

As avid fans of the Morgan and Wong writing team may have already noticed, it isn't unusual for veterans of their series *Space: Above and Beyond* to appear in episodes of *The X-Files* filmed during the fourth season. Though Tucker Smallwood is one such veteran, his filmography reflects the interesting career he's enjoyed away from Ten-Thirteen and Hard Eight productions.

Bio-Dome (1996) – Gates
Black Sheep (1996) – Election Analyst
Tom Clancy's SSN (1996) – Admiral Jeb Thomas
"Babylon 5" [Matters of Honor] (1995) – David Endawi
"Space: Above and Beyond" (1995) – Commodore Ross
Aurora: Operation Intercept (1995) – Agent
"Seinfeld" [The Parking Garage] (1991) – Man in Mercedes
"Seinfeld" [The Pen] (1991) – Photographer
Presumed Innocent (1990) – Det. Harold Greer
Turk 182 (1985) Reporter
The Cotton Club (1984) – Kid Griffin
"For Ladies Only!" (1981) – Tornado

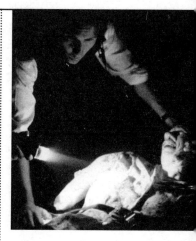

Hard to believe "Ma Peacock" could ever play a dancer!

X BLOOPER! If Mrs. Peacock suffered from the genetically-inheritable inability to feel pain, why was she screaming her head off in the opening scenes while giving birth to her deformed child? Childbirth, while certainly more "uncomfortable" than "making breakfast," probably doesn't rate quite as high as having your arm ripped off!

X Adrian Hughes, aka Sherman Peacock, has appeared in other film and television roles, but he is perhaps most infamous in X-Philedom as the man with whom Gillian Anderson is suspected of having a fling during a trip to Great Britain before he was accused of rape by several women.

that most viewers would find disturbing." She grins. "Well, that and watching the whole thing with that song playing in the background!"

Tony Murray, a long-time member of the Coalition for Quality Broadcasting, and a big fan of the show, suggested the warning may have been included because, "This episode wasn't really about an X-file at all. Most people understand that the MOWs [Monsters of the Week] don't actually exist outside of their TVs, but, there was nothing paranormal about the Peacock brothers. They were bizarre, but, if you ignore all the DNA malarky, they were just humans with some nasty genetic problems and a pretty severe case of anti-social behaviour. Some viewers might have found that aspect disturbing. Instead of a frozen alien fetus getting stuck in cold storage, a human child was being buried alive. It makes a difference."

It certainly did to Carolyn MacIsaccs who chairs the Canadian Genetic Disorders Association. "I personally find it unsettling that a large American television network thinks this program rated a warning but that 'specials' like *When Animals Attack*! and all those other 'reality-based' items that FOX runs

X And just who is the Bruno Hauptmann of Mulder's joking aside? The man convicted of murdering the Lindbergh baby. The kidnapping-murder of the son of aviation ace Charles Lindbergh is an oddity, even for the American law enforcement community, and among the many "irregularities" of the kidnapping investigation

was the suspicion that rubber hoses might have been employed in the collection of evidence and confessions.

In yet another irony, Hauptmann, who was executed in 1936, didn't actually receive the death penalty for either kidnapping or murder. You see, in New Jersey, where the kidnapping was committed, kidnapping wasn't a capital offense and,

although Hauptmann may well have been responsible for the child's death, the prosecutors couldn't make a case for the *intent* to murder.

It appears quite likely Charles Augustus Lindbergh Jr. died accidentally during the kidnapping. In yet another example of the bizarre twists of American justice, and the somewhat questionable tactics of both the FBI and a

judicial system that seemed more interested in public opinions than justice, Bruno Hauptmann was indirectly executed for the theft of the child's pyjamas – which he just happened to be wearing at the time. The justification? Theft of some flannel nightwear, not kidnapping, upped the charges against Hauptmann to a *felony* murder.

It's hard to believe that even a mother could love these guys!

X Music lovers should note that the version of "Wonderful! Wonderful!" in this episode was sung by Kenny James, not Johnny Mathis who made it a huge success in 1957.

don't! What was it they had on last week? *The Most Dangerous Shootouts* or something like that? Anyway, those items, which everyone *knows* are taken from real video footage and which run even earlier in the evening, when it's more likely that younger viewers would be watching, don't have any warnings while this one fictional episode did? I mean, I watched the show. It was scary, but hardly any more gory than dozens of other things on television. Why would the only unusual feature, the genetic disorders, rate special warnings?"

A psychologist in London, Dwayne Smythe, thinks the extreme reactions to the airing of "Home" had little to do with the violence and much more to do with the number of societal taboos the episode explored. "In less than an hour, 'Home' challenged its audience to think about a lot of scary issues. Incest. Infanticide. The way humanity has traditionally treated those who were physically different. Any *one* of those topics can take up an entire full-length film. Packing so many emotionally explosive issues into forty-seven minutes is like taking your audience and forcing them off one roller coaster and onto another without stop."

X BLOOPER! This episode delivers yet more un-evidence of Mulder's on-again-off-again color-blindness. When Scully asks if there's any genetic conditions floating about in the Mulder family, his riposte is, "Aside from the need for corrective lenses and a tendency to be abducted by extraterrestrials involved in an international government conspiracy, the Mulder family passes genetic muster." Absolutely no mention of the genetically-inherited red-green color blindness.

WRITTEN BY: Glen Morgan and
    James Wong
DIRECTED BY: Kim Manners
ORIGINAL PRODUCTION
    NUMBER: 4X03
ORIGINAL US AIR DATE: 10/11/96

GUEST CAST

SHERIFF ANDY TAYLOR
    Tucker Smallwood
MRS. BARBARA TAYLOR
    Judith Maxie
DEPUTY BARNEY PASTER
    Sebastian Spence
MRS. PEACOCK
    Karin Konoval
EDMUND PEACOCK
    Chris Norris
GEORGE PEACOCK
    John Trottier
SHERMAN PEACOCK
    Adrian Hughes
THE BATTER
    Cory Frye
THE CATCHER
    Neil Denis
THE PITCHER
    Douglas Smith

DEATH TOLL

2 MEN: 1 bludgeoned to death,
    1 impaled
1 WOMAN: bludgeoned to death
1 CHILD: (undetermined sex) buried
    alive

Scully and Mulder as we've never seen them before.

In Toronto, a small cyber cafe known locally as The Spot has become the defacto meeting place for a group of *The X-Files*'s most devoted – and critical – fans. Not surprisingly, "Home" generated heated debate. Even amid accusations of "gratuitous violence," however, was an admittedly reluctant admiration for "hitting viewers where they live."

Carly Farewell, who hits The Spot every Sunday evening to watch her favorite program on a four-foot screen, was frankly amazed by the condemnation. "Sure some scenes were a bit over the top – I personally *hated* the scene when Mama got hungry – but, I didn't see anyone racing for the bathroom or leaving because they were offended or even hiding behind their fingers, all of which happened when I saw *Deliverance* at the movie theatre."

Whether it was loved or loathed, "Home" will be a hard episode to forget.

CODE NAME:

"Teliko"

Case: XF-4X04-10-18-96

X CATCH IT? Once again, the catch phrase "THE TRUTH IS OUT THERE" was dropped from the opening sequence, this time in favor of "DECEIVE INVEIGLE OBFUSCATE," proving the joke currently circulating at conventions that *The X-Files* is the only program that should come with a dictionary instead of a viewer's guide.

EYEWITNESS STATEMENT

"All new truths begin as heresies and end as superstitions. We fear the unknown so we reduce it to the terms that are most familiar to us, whether that's a folktale, or a disease, or . . . a conspiracy."

Special Agent Fox Mulder

CASE SUMMARY

Young black men are dying in Philadelphia. Their bodies, stripped of essential chemicals, appear more the victim of disease than foul play – at least to the Center for Disease Control, and to Scully. Mulder isn't so sure and, while Scully hunts down a medical demon, Mulder searches for a much more literal one that's so far remained hidden in the realms of folklore.

CASE HISTORY
The Monster Under The Bed

Ask twenty children what's lurking under their beds when the lights go out and you'll immediately be swamped with twenty versions of the Bogeyman. Like crime scene witnesses, no two children will be able to provide matching descriptions of this cryptozoological oddity, but, as any two kids will also tell you, the details don't matter in the dark.

So what if North American Bogeymen are green with a tendency to sliminess while their compatriots in Norway wrap themselves in the blacks and grays of night and have disjoint arms and legs that look – and feel – like old roots and tree branches? It's what they *do*, not what they look like, that makes them Bogeymen. Regardless of their home town, Bogeymen have one responsibility, namely to grab the ankles of unwary little children silly enough to creep from under their covers. Luckily for children everywhere, even if their parents have neglected to educate their offspring on the hazards of creatures living under beds, there's always *someone* able and willing to pass the story on to those who don't like to stay in bed.

Like the Bogeyman, who crosses language and political borders with equal ease, there's a West African figure that, though known by a multitude of names, also serves a singular purpose. Whether he's called the Sumabra, the Kinto Loat, the Web Walker, the Gaddy Defant, or as in the story created for this episode, the Teliko, the white body- and soul-snatchers have been striding through a distinct set of folktales, the slaver stories, since African coastal communities were first raided to provide slaves for the labour-poor New World.

The Gaddy Defant who, like the Teliko, seemed to decide there were greener pastures in the Americas than West Africa, still makes its appearances in stories from Haiti and Puerto Rico. According to legend, the Gaddy Defant was a ghostly presence, "paler than ivory," capable of snatching away the children of mothers who failed to closely supervise their small children. It swept up and down the coast in its ghost ship, adding to its horde whenever possible. The shrieks heard during storms were, of course, the unending lament of its victims who were doomed never to return to their homeland. The Gaddy Defant seldom appeared in daylight, preferring to "hide its white face" until darkness concealed him. It, too, could hide in the smallest crevice and the women were encouraged to sweep out every nook of their homes during the bright daylight hours when the Gaddy Defant was at its weakest, then remain vigilant through the night to prevent its return.

The Sumabra of Gabon could easily provide the model for yet another part of the story Mulder recounts to Scully, that of the "Lost Tribe." Unlike the Teliko that takes up residence in Philadelphia, the Sumabra are more sociable "white devils." Hunting in packs, and described as "hordes" in most of the children's stories, the Sumabra would descend on the village they'd targeted, running around it at great speed, creating a mighty gale, to prevent anyone from escaping and then darting in and out as individuals to carry off whichever members of the tribe took their fancy. Those lost quickly turned as pale as their captors and would even begin raiding their former homes and leading their new masters deeper into the interior to ravage neighbouring villages.

The legends also warned children of Sumabrain villages to be found deep in the hills or hidden in the darkest parts of the

THESE ARE THE EASY ONES! TAKE A SINGLE POINT FOR EACH CORRECT ANSWER.

1. Which embassy does Mulder visit?

2. Where did Aboah hide his blowpipe?

3. What's the common name for the plant whose seed Mulder and Pendrell found in some Hair and Fibre evidence?

4. What building was to be erected on Aboah's hiding place in Liberty Plaza?

5. Where did the plane carrying the Teliko land?

THESE WILL MAKE YOU THINK, SO GIVE YOURSELF TWO POINTS FOR A CORRECT RESPONSE.

6. Name the Philadelphia representative of the Center for Disease Control.

7. What case number does Scully quote during the autopsy of Owen Sanders?

8. What's Samuel Aboah's address?

9. What did Aboah use as a getaway vehicle to escape his hospital room?

10. What gland did Aboah not have?

4

Answers

KEEP TRACK OF YOUR TOTAL SCORE.
SEE WHERE YOU'D END UP IN THE
X-FILEAN WORLD OF HIERARCHIES,
SHADOW GOVERNMENTS,
AND CONSPIRACIES.

ONE POINTERS:

1. The Embassy for Burkina Faso.

2. Down his own throat.

3. It was a passion flower.

4. The Museum of Independence.

5. John F. Kennedy International Airport, New York City.

TWO POINTERS:

6. Dr. Simon Bruin.

7. 2139318537.

8. 500 Dermott Avenue, Apt. 23, Philadelphia.

9. A very small cart.
He hid in the drawer.

10. A pituitary gland.

YOUR SCORE _____

forests. Unlike the Sumabra themselves, their villages, usually found deserted, were delightful. Succulent meals simmered over cooking fires. Verdant garden patches promised plenty of food for the future. Stores of honey lured greedy children into sturdy homes. Music floated on the air in Sumabra's glades.

At nightfall, however, things change – swiftly. The music turns to moans, the honey to bitter tree sap. As the Sumabra roar up from crevices in the ground, a choking stench accompanies them and the plentiful food rots before the terrified visitor's eyes as the Sumabra's vicious hunt begins again.

Any village courageous enough, or lucky enough, to make an effective stand against the Sumabra, however, were treated to rather unusual sights. According to the legend, if the Sumabra couldn't claim new victims before sunrise, or were caught and forced to sit out in the daylight, the bleached Sumabran would regain his healthy color and be free to return to his village. For the oldest Sumabran, for whom there was no hope, the end was less pleasant as the unfortunate captive burst into flame and, rising in the smoke, become a true creature of the air.

In both the Gaddy Defant and the Sumabra tales, the thieving spirits were forced to take solid, basically human shapes before claiming their victims. The Web Crawlers, while fitting all the classic elements of a slaver story, are unique for their startling portrayal of the slavers. Instead of familiarly shaped, but alien in habit and coloration, the Web Crawlers' traditional description is of a massive, bloated spider that lures children deeper into the forests by leaving sweet drops of a honey-like substance trailing behind it. Once the naive child is too far away to attract an adult's attention, thick strands of webbing drop from above, quickly followed by the spider who flings a larger section of prepared webbing over the child before bundling up the struggling youngster to add to its larder. The only hint of these creatures' human roots is found in the bleached head each spider-spirit will have hanging from somewhere on its body. When not busy munching on children, the spider entertains itself by rolling the head about, stroking it with the tips of its legs before settling down around it. As might be expected, destroying the head destroys the monster's power, making it possible for the creature to be killed by a determined village using only normal weapons.

Horrid as the Web Crawlers seem, and I for one wouldn't want to find one under my bed, an even more horrific creature stalks West Africa's oral folklore – the Kinto Loat. This

NOTEBOOK

Guest Filmography: Carl Lumbly

"The Ditchdigger's Daughter" (1997) – Donald

American Dream – Cal

"M.A.N.T.I.S." (1994 – 95) – Dr. Miles Hawkins

"Cagney & Lacey: The Return" (1994) – Marcus Petrie

"On Promised Land" (1994) – Floyd

"Out of Darkness" (1994) – Addison

"Going to Extremes" (1992) – Dr. Norris

"Back to the Streets of San Francisco" (1992) – Charlie Walker

South Central (1992) – Ali

Eyes of a Witness (1991) – Mambulu

Pacific Heights (1990) – Lou Baker

To Sleep With Anger (1990) – Junior

Everybody's All-American (1988) – Narvel Blue

The Bedroom Window (1987) – Quirke

"Conspiracy: The Trial of the Chicago 8" (1987) – Bobby Seale

The Adventures of Buckaroo Banzai Across the 8th Dimension (1984) – John Parker

"Cagney & Lacey" (1981–1982) – Det. Marcus Petrie

X Many fans complained that "Teliko" was nothing more than a poor imitation of "Squeeze" and its sequel "Tooms," with a little folklore throw in. But it's an indication of how *The X-Files* audience has grown when one realizes that this "mediocre" episode actually drew nearly twice the audience that "Squeeze" did on its first appearance – the supposedly superior episode and an acknowledged classic.

Though Mulder and Pendrell are surprised to find the seed of a rare plant in Philadelphia, purely natural conditions have, from time to time, resulted in some rather bizarre migrations. In 1986, a tropical storm blew through the Caribbean and across the southern United States. Several weeks later, an ornithologist at a university in Newfoundland was rather startled by the appearance of a local man carrying a brilliant pink flamingo! When Krakatoa blew up just over a hundred years ago, it wasn't just smoke and fumes that got carried away on the resultant heat wave. The blast sent hundreds of thousands of fern spores high into the atmosphere where they were caught up by the prevailing trade winds. Even now, observers will occasionally spot the odd non-indigenous fern sprouting thousands of miles away in the midst of an otherwise perfectly ordinary grouping of plants. One such "alien" is known to have appeared in a garden in Kensington as late as 1993.

pale, wraith-like killer appears as a skeleton loosely covered by pale skin that rustles with each movement. Paler hair floats out around its bony shoulders. Watery blue eyes paralyse its victims. Quills spit from its mouth carry poison and, once caught, there's no escape for its miserable victims. Though the Kinto Loat continuously plucks flesh from their bodies to feed itself, it never takes enough at one time to kill the victim. The victim, despite its complete lack of physical restraints, simply can't run away. The only way to slow the progress of the poison carried by the Kinto Loat's quills is to ingest the sweat of the monster's own body. Without this disgusting antidote, the victim dies an excruciating death then rises again as one of the Kinto Loat. To avoid that fate, to keep themselves from one day finding themselves feasting on their children, the Kinto Loat's sad victims will trail along in its wake offering up their own flesh to share in a temporary respite from yet further horrors.

Just as a child cares little for the color of it's own Bogeymen, however, the particulars of any region's "Teliko" don't really matter. What does matter, to the cultures who create the myth and to those who study them in an attempt to understand human experience, is the consistencies among the versions. Slaving occurred over hundreds of miles of coastline, affected dozens of disconnected social groups, yet its history was, compared to the long African oral history, relatively short. Still, the slaver legends persist, even in the absence of raiders, following their creators to Haiti, Puerto Rico, Jamaica, and, of course, the United States.

In every case, the enemy, the alien, the "other," is visibly different from the population he ravages. Pale skin, blond hair, and eyes with pupils that remain visible even at a distance all provide stark contrasts to the West African populations who produced them. While even such exceedingly rare traits would occasionally arise from naturally occurring albinism, tales of

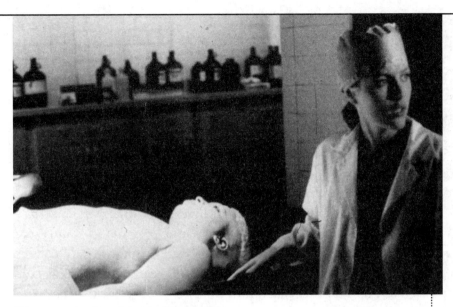

All those caps and masks must play hell with the hairdressing.

white monsters remained scarce until a concrete enemy in the form of western Europeans began regular raids. Yet, by almost immediately integrating this new threat into their existing mythos, many communities presented a remarkably concerted defence in short order – much to the invader's surprise. Given a choice between an already "hardened" target and a less prepared village, slavers would raid a little further afield rather than waste time and effort on more vigilant tribes.

And, despite the seemingly fantastic abilities attributed to the various "Telikos," most tales are firmly rooted in fact. The slavers *could* sweep ahead of the winds with boats capable of easily outstripping the primitive sea-going vessels of the native West African population. The tactics attributed to the Sumabra, with minor differences, do indeed reflect several of the ways slavers separated villagers from one another. One was to quietly sneak into the woods surrounding a village where they'd make sufficient noise to seriously alarm a sleeping community while effectively hiding the number of attackers. As the village rushed from side to side to meet an attack that quickly melted back into the woods, slavers on the opposite side would

CASE CREDITS

WRITTEN BY: Howard Gordon
DIRECTED BY: James Charleston
ORIGINAL PRODUCTION
   NUMBER: 4X04
ORIGINAL US AIR DATE: 10/18/96

GUEST CAST

ASSISTANT DIRECTOR WALTER
S. SKINNER
   Mitch Pileggi
AGENT PENDRELL
   Brendan Beiser
MARITA COVARRUBIAS
   Laurie Holden
BUSINESSMAN
   Don Stewart
SEAT MATE
   Geoffrey Ayi-Bonte
FLIGHT ATTENDANT
   Maxine Guess
SAMUEL ABOAH
   Willie Amakye
DR. SIMON BRUIN
   Bob Morrisey
MARCUS DUFF
   Carl Lumbly
ALFRED KITTEL
   Dexter Bell
DIABRIA
   Zakes Mokae
LT. MADSEN
   Sean Campbell

DEATH TOLL

2 MEN: "de-melanized"
4 men die of "de-melanization" in
   events prior to opening scene

dart in and grab the unprotected. Even the Sumabran villages take on some semblance of reality when readers realize that, in cases where outright kidnapping wouldn't do, some slavers set up "trading posts" which were little more than fronts to lure the trusting locals away from the immediate vicinity of their homes. Even the spider silk thrown by the Web Crawlers bears an uncanny resemblance to the nets some slavers used to entangle groups of Africans until several kidnappers could sort out which of the group they wanted. That the Kinto Loat should appear the most horrific of all the monsters is likely as no surprise either as the Kinto Loat represented in folktale the all too real turncoats who, for pay, would lead the slavers to villages that might otherwise have been passed by.

CODE NAME:

"The field where I died"

Case: XF-4X05-11-03-96

CASE SUMMARY

While investigating a cult suspected of stock-piling illegal weapons, Mulder finds himself "remembering" things he could never have known. For him, it falls into place when he meets their mysterious informant, Sidney, who turns out to be a woman – and a wife of the cult's leader. Mulder suspects "Sidney" is one of the woman's past lives; Scully has a suggestion only slightly less exotic – Multiple Personality Syndrome. Regardless, however, they have only hours to find the evidence needed to shut down a compound all too likely to self-destruct.

CASE HISTORY
The FBI and Cults: A History of Failure

Regardless of what you may think of past lives, regression hypnosis, or false memory syndrome, "The Field Where I Died" was perhaps the most technically, and historically, accurate episode ever produced on *The X-Files*. Skinner was sweating. The FBI and the Bureau of Alcohol, Tobacco and Firearms scrapped with each other and among themselves at the least provocation. And, in a compound that could easily have been Jim Jones's Jonestown or David Koresh's Mt. Carmel, Vernon Ephesian's Temple of the Seven Stars, complete with bunkers and bolt holes, would have made any apocalyptic cultist feel right at home.

In other words, a perfectly legitimate representation of the tension-filled scenario that had already been acted out in Waco, Texas, and in a self-made community called Jonestown in Guyana. Like "The Field Where I Died," both these real-life tales really begin with a charismatic leader, a religious front, and the victims who'll die for their beliefs.

The slaughter carried out in a compound hacked out of the Guyanese bush was actually set in motion some distance away in California when the self-styled Reverend Jim Jones, a devoted Marxist if a rather intemperate Christian, founded the People's Temple. His "flock" were the minority immigrants and illegal aliens. His prophetic messages promised equality before God, and, if they were devout enough, a reflection of that equality while still members of the material world. While no one disputed the validity of his ministry, despite the fact that the good Reverend wasn't actually an ordained minister in any church – not even his own – many failed to see how allowing his followers to live in ever reduced circumstances while he himself enjoyed an inversely-related amount of wealth could make them more "equal." Regardless of the apparent discrepancies between his message and his bank statements, Jones mounted a singularly successful campaign portraying himself as a defender of civil rights and the down-trodden. He was personally instrumental in raising millions of dollars which the donators believed would be used to stage protests and lobby governments for equal rights.

Things inside Jim Jones's church weren't as cheery as he made them appear. Like the fictional Vernon Ephesian, Jim Jones demanded immediate and total submission from his followers. To keep any member who might have second thoughts from leaving, Jones encouraged violent "encounter" sessions between any free-thinkers and the remainder of the flock. Beatings, with and without wooden paddles, were a daily affair. The majority of his followers, however, had little energy for mutiny after the demanding schedules, often as much as nineteen hours of hard labor a day, through which Jim Jones and his senior church "officials" put back-sliding congregants. From the information provided by those members who did manage to free themselves, it seems all too likely that clandestine doping quickly became a regular aspect of the hold Jones maintained over his growing church.

Needless to say, these tactics wouldn't remain a secret for long and, for much of 1977, The People's Temple remained

5

THESE ARE THE EASY ONES! TAKE A SINGLE POINT FOR EACH CORRECT ANSWER.

1. Which Biblical book did Ephesian constantly quote?

2. What condition does Scully believe explains Melissa's "memories"?

3. Which of Melissa's alter-egos contacted federal agents?

4. What did Vernon Ephesian call his church?

5. What was the name of Melissa's young alter-ego?

THESE WILL MAKE YOU THINK, SO GIVE YOURSELF TWO POINTS FOR A CORRECT RESPONSE.

6. What was Vernon Ephesian's original name?

7. By what name did Mulder identify himself under hypnosis?

8. Which of the many incidents that Scully and Mulder have shared did Scully decide she could have "lived without"?

9. How did Ephesian's followers kill themselves?

10. Where did "Sarah Kavanaugh" say the weapons were stored?

Answers

KEEP TRACK OF YOUR TOTAL SCORE.
SEE WHERE YOU'D END UP IN THE
X-FILEAN WORLD OF HIERARCHIES,
SHADOW GOVERNMENTS,
AND CONSPIRACIES.

ONE POINTERS:

1. Revelations.

2. Multiple Personality Syndrome.

3. Sidney.

4. The Temple of the Seven Stars.

5. Lily.

TWO POINTERS:

6. Vernon Warren.

7. Sullivan Biddle.

8. Their encounter with the Flukeman.

9. Poison.

10. In an underground Civil War bunker.

YOUR SCORE: _____

closely scrutinized. As investigators began exploring charges of financial irregularity, Jones was real-estate shopping. In the depths of a Guyanese jungle, he found his church's next home. With just over twelve hundred of his most fanatical, or desperate, membership behind him, Jones simply moved his religious community out of the United States and away from any possibility of criminal investigation – or so he believed.

Though Jones continued to promote himself and his new paradise-on-earth, Jonestown, it was becoming harder to avoid the accusations of law enforcement officials and ex-sheep. During the fall of 1978, dozens of calls, many claiming, as Sidney would in "The Field Where I Died," that American children were being held against their will and that full-scale child abuse was becoming the *status quo*, flooded into the offices of both legal and journalistic investigators.

On November 18, 1978, Leo Ryan and four reporters arrived at the tiny airstrip servicing Jonestown. It didn't take long to determine that Jones's devoted followers were living in squalor. Fourteen to sixteen people were jammed into each tiny, waterless, powerless hut. Some had no hut at all. Not even the surrounding jungle could provide shelter as it teemed with wildlife the Temple's membership had no defences against. Jones had effectively isolated them from any aid and those running Jonestown weren't about to let any more information reach the public. The Ryan party never made it back to their plane. They were massacred on the runway.

When a full detachment of Guyanan troops and yet another American team landed on the 20th, there were few left to save. Those who had survived, most in deep shock, told of suicide and murder. Though it took weeks to sort through everything, and everyone, from the Jonestown commune, the numbers were appalling. Some two hundred people had voluntarily swallowed potassium cyanide, as well as a multitude of prescription tranquillizers and narcotics, all dissolved in orange drink crystals. Witnesses reported that hundreds more, especially children, had the drink forced on them. When submission came too slowly, the Temple's leaders used some of the nearly forty weapons stashed around the compound to force obedience. If that wasn't sufficient inducement, the stragglers were shot where they stood. Coroners' reports eventually accounted for 917 victims, over six hundred of which died from beatings or gunshot wounds.

Among those dead was Jim Jones, member of the American Communist Party, avowed Marxist, personal owner of some $5,000,000, controller of another $15,000,000, and, in his later days, firm believer in the fact that he was Lenin. He had a bullet in his head. His dying words are reported to have been "Mother, mother."

Though he actually believed in none of the religious philosophy he spouted, Jones created the Apocalypse he'd preached for the last twenty-nine years, the Armageddon sermons he'd passed on to the thousands of congregants he'd amassed since opening his first church when he was just eighteen. Whether the arrival of Congressman Ryan precipitated the mass murder-suicide can't be known, but, as Jones's many delusions were known to include the notion that the CIA was poisoning his provisions, the mix of Apocalyptic prophesy and heavy government investigation was likely doomed to failure.

Still, the disaster at Jonestown was, in many ways, a unique situation for law enforcement. Certainly, there were, and are, militant churches throughout the United States. But until Jim Jones spurred his followers to their deaths, no one really knew the power wielded by a charismatic religious leader.

There was, however, no such excuse when BATF and FBI agents surrounded another commune just outside Waco, Texas. Once again, they confronted a religious compound known to be heavily armed. Once again, the followers had

X CATCH IT? While Scully's doctor-cum-agent background is brought up in practically every episode, few writers seem to remember that it's *Mulder* who has the psychology degree! In "The Field Where I Died," even Skinner, who we assume has read Mulder's file at some point, turns to Scully to determine if multiple personalities are theoretically possible. The Mulder character gets something of his own back when he caustically quotes chapter and verse of the DSM-VI as easily as Scully tosses out the name of rare syndromes.

clearly chosen to ignore the social dictates which might have weakened the commitment of any common criminals who found themselves under siege. Once again, they faced a charismatic religious leader. This time, it was David Koresh. This time, his followers weren't trying to run away. Instead, they dug in deep and hard, defying the federal agents camped

NOTEBOOK

Guest Filmography: Kristen Cloke

Another of the actors who appeared on a Morgan and Wong-written episode of *The X-Files* after appearing on the writing team's *Space: Above and Beyond*, Kristen Cloke is a veteran television performer though her talents may well have been best displayed in "The Field Where I Died" where she played not one but four completely separate personalities.

The Rage

"Winnetka Road" (1994)

"One West Waikiki" (1994)

"Mother of the Bride" (1993)

"JA Part of the Family" (1993)

"Mad About You" (1992)

Caged Fear (1992)

Stay Tuned (1992)

"Silk Stalkings" (1991)

The Marrying Man (1991)

Megaville (1990)

"Quantum Leap" (1989)

"Doogie Howser, M.D." (1989)

"Dead John" (1988)

"Murder, She Wrote" (1984)

"Cheers" (1982)

outside their doors to take on the power of prophesy, and, unlike Jim Jones's fly-by-night ministry, the Branch Davidians had a long history binding them together.

Long before David Koresh, who like the fictional Ephesian was also originally named Vernon, arrived on the scene, the Davidians had been led by several inspired, if totalitarian, visionaries. In 1929, Victor Houteff, who claimed his church, the Seventh Day Adventists, was too soft, too lenient, gathered together a group of hard-core supporters and broke away to form the Davidian Adventists. Leaning strongly towards an Apocalyptic interpretation of biblical literature, Houteff strictly enforced theological and personal discipline within the ranks of his new church. Punishment came quickly and severely within the membership, but, in many ways, the Davidian Adventists made little impact on those around them, withdrawing even further from public awareness when Houteff bought a 189-acre ranch just outside Waco, called it Mount Carmel, and retreated inside with his "faithful." The site attracted a steady, but small, number of new adherents as time passed, but, when Houteff died in 1955, little had changed in the new sect's first twenty-five years.

Wife Florence, who inherited her husband's ministry, made changes. Within two years of burying her husband, Florence sold off the first estate to buy a new, bigger location on the other side of town. It, too, was called Mount Carmel, but Florence Houteff began subtly altering the text of the Davidian Adventists's message. It seems Florence fancied herself a prophetess. Looking into the future for her followers, she predicted that the Apocalypse wasn't just "near," it was imminent. According to her insights and beliefs, the beginning of the end would come in April or May of 1959. As the spring days of 1959 passed peacefully, Vernon Howell, later David Koresh, was born, Lois and Ben Roden eased the tottering Florence out of her leadership, and as the world failed to disappear in fire and

X Some of the most beautiful dialogue of this episode, namely Mulder's soliloquy, which opens and closes "The Field Where I Died," was actually written by Robert Browning. The poem is *Paracelsus*. If you'd like to read the entire work, take an entire afternoon and really enjoy it, all 4100-plus lines.

X Anyone who thought "Sullivan Biddle" sounded vaguely familiar might have been remembering a Civil War special by Ken Burns in which a soldier named Major Sullivan Ballou writes a memorably romantic letter to his wife, Sarah.

brimstone, a significant number of Davidian Adventists lost their faith and walked away from Mount Carmel.

With old Florence safely out of the way and unlikely to return from her semi-enforced religious seclusion, the Rodens quickly set about reviving their flagging church. Now known as the Branch Davidians, the church became an active recruiter of young people, wealthy people, and people in positions of influence. Under Lois and Ben's careful tending, the church shed some of its previous associations with Apocalyptic theology, returning to a slightly more conventional path, a path that would eventually cross that of Vernon Howell.

Ben Roden died in 1981. Thirty-year-old Vernon Howell arrived in 1985 and wasted no time striking up a sexual relationship with Ben's then sixty-seven-year-old widow. The Rodens' son, George, made no uproar about his mother's new partner until, after her death in 1986, the young upstart now known as David Koresh claimed leadership of the church for himself instead of allowing George, the patient princeling in waiting, to step into his mother's shoes. Though few clear-cut records of this tumultuous period were made, the in-fighting was said to be vicious and ended with George Roden in a mental institution and David Koresh with undisputed leadership of the Branch Davidians.

Now things changed quickly.

Like "The Field Where I Died"'s Vernon Ephesian, David Koresh believed in polygamy. In addition to his affair with Lois, Koresh took his first wife, Rachel, only fourteen at the time, in 1984. Rachel was pregnant before she turned fifteen. Shortly after Lois's death, he married Rachel's younger sister, twelve-year-old Michelle. It was these two marriages that would start the investigation in child sexual abuse among the Davidians. He married three more times in the next year – each time to a woman less than half his own young age. In 1989, inspired by visions and the Book of Revelations, Koresh ordered all members of the sect to become celibate – all members *except* himself as God's Chosen One and His Chosen Wives.

Like Vernon Ephesian, Koresh never allowed the commune's children to leave. Instead, David Koresh insisted the children be raised in the commune. Each of his wives was to participate in the rearing of all his children, children he, too, called The Children of God.

He stressed the Branch Davidians' need for self-sufficiency and, quoting as needed from botched versions of Revelations and the Book of Daniel, unsurprising favorites among those prophets who fancy an explosive end to the world, urged the group to stockpile weapons to be used as their defence against the "unbelievers" when the Day of Judgement arrived. Koresh also began preaching a philosophy of armed resistance to any and all authorities other than himself. Claiming divine knowledge, Koresh exempted himself from the authority and decisions of those without his unique insight. Like Jones and like Ephesian, Koresh severed his community's ties to the outside world, threatening and physically abusing those who would attempt to leave.

For all Koresh's seemingly undeniable will, however, it quickly became apparent that he couldn't control the information leaking out to law enforcement. The Davidians had their own version of Sidney.

On February 28, 1993, after numerous tip-offs, BATF agents tried to force their way onto the Davidian compound. The Davidians, answering their leader's call to acknowledge no outside authority, desperately fought off what they considered an invasion. In the process, four of the twenty-six BATF agents died, six Davidians died, and nearly a dozen others sustained gunshot wounds. In the end, the BATF agents were still outside and the Davidians were even more strongly united in their belief that the government was the enemy. The FBI was called in and the situation, in many ways, went from bad to worse.

Philes who've been wondering if Mulder isn't just latently suicidal didn't find much evidence to contradict that in this episode!

CASE CREDITS

WRITTEN BY: Glen Morgan and
    James Wong
DIRECTED BY: Rob Bowman
ORIGINAL PRODUCTION
    NUMBER: 4X05
ORIGINAL US AIR DATE: 11/03/96

GUEST CAST

ASSISTANT DIRECTOR WALTER S.
SKINNER
    Mitch Pileggi
BATF AGENT
    Michael Dobson
AGENT RIGGINS
    Anthony Harrison
MELISSA RIEDAL-EPHESIAN
    Kristen Cloke
VERNON EPHESIAN
    Michael Massee
MIGHTY MAN
    Douglas Roy Dack
HARBAUGH
    Doug Abrahams
THE ATTORNEY
    Les Gallagher
THE THERAPIST
    Donna White

DEATH TOLL

More than 50 men, women and
    children, by poison

In the investigation that was to follow, several items became clear.

A virtual turf-war raged between the BATF agents who'd originally targeted the Waco compound and the FBI agents called in to assist.

Even among the FBI agents, two distinct groups, the negotiators and the rescue team, formed and continued to work against one another's efforts throughout the stand-off. On the night after the negotiators had arranged the release of a number of women and children, the rescue team, a tactics unit, rewarded the Davidians for their co-operation by blaring rock music into the compound all night! Despite complaints from both groups, no one stepped in to enforce an action plan.

The new Attorney General, Janet Reno, who wasn't even in office when the BATF assault failed, was fed misleading information about "baby beaters." Reno, known for her previous stands on children's issues, had just arrived in Washington and had, as yet, absolutely no independent hierarchy of information by which to judge the situation.

When Reno asked about the risks posed by the CS gas proposed as an agent to "soften" the Waco target, she once again received incomplete, if not outright false, information. She was not informed of the risk the gas posed to children or to the pregnant women inside the compound. The Davidians, however, probably did know and, knowing, would have interpreted the "softening" tactics much differently than Reno.

With such a damning history, a history recreated from the bright orange drink carrying the Ephesians' poison to the claustrophobically insular nature of the compounds to the presence of hidden bunkers during "The Field Where I Died," it wouldn't have taken any paranormal ability to predict the outcome at the Temple of the Seven Stars.

CODE NAME:

"Sanguinarium"

Case: XF-4X06-11-10-96

EYEWITNESS STATEMENT

"Oh, there's magic going on here, Mulder, only it's being done with silicon, collagen and a well-placed scalpel!"

Special Agent Dana Scully

CASE SUMMARY

When patients on a plastic surgery unit are murdered by their own physicians – who claim to have been "possessed" as they mutilated their victims – Mulder and Scully must discover if it's bad medicine or black magic behind the deaths. That task is made more difficult by the presence of a nurse with an agenda all her own, and one of the doctors as her own target.

CASE HISTORY
There's Many A Slip

An amazing 83 per cent of all Americans have been hospitalized at some point in their lives, most for invasive surgery of some type or another, and world-wide figures indicate that residents of Great Britain, India, China and Japan are twice as likely to spend three or more days in a hospital than their parents were. We aren't necessarily any sicker, but it seems we're willing to undergo some pretty drastic procedures almost at the drop of a hat. Even after excluding all plastic and aesthetic surgeries, we're still ten times as likely to end up under the knife as our grandparents. It seems that, as modern surgical procedures come to be perceived as safer and more reliable, we're more willing to take risks with ourselves.

Take carpal tunnel syndrome as an example. Twenty-five years ago, someone suffering from the painful hand-wrist ailment would receive little or no medical treatment other than a prescription for Aspirin and the admonition to rest the affected hand or hands as much as possible. Today, thousands of people receive surgical relief each month. It appears that people like my grandfather, who share the firm conviction that hospitals are places where people go to die, are quickly becoming a small minority in the general population.

Unfortunately for the rest of us, he – and a Harvard University study – may be right!

In 1991, the researchers at Harvard concluded that some 86,000 Americans die *every year* from negligence in American hospitals. Hundreds of thousands are maimed, injured, or infected with further diseases. While my grandfather would shrug that off as no more than he'd expected, it's a rather sobering thought for most people when we realize that American hospitals are generally considered to be some of the best health care facilities in the world!

Cases like that of Betsy Lehman, however, could quickly gain converts for my grandfather's pessimistic prognosis on hospitals in general. Betsy Lehman, who'd worked as a health reporter for the *Boston Globe* for over a decade, probably figured she knew all the risks when she was checked into the Dana-Farber Cancer Institute, ironically an affiliate of the same university which just a few years ago put out the startling report on the state of American hospitals. Ms. Lehman knew her breast cancer was in a dangerously advanced stage and she would certainly have studied both the experimental treatment being offered to her and the staff who would be administering it before putting herself at the mercy of the Institute. Still, in spite of all her precautions, Betsy Lehman, just 39-years-old, died in a respected treatment facility, not of breast cancer, but of a drug overdose! Instead of receiving the powerful drugs in even distributions over her anticipated four-day stay, Betsy Lehman received the entire dosage at once. She never had a chance against such a massive assault on her system by drugs that are normally dispensed at levels already dangerously close to lethal.

When the American Hospital Advisory Committee undertook a study of prescription errors between 1992 and 1994, they expected to see some irregularities. Doctors, nurses and pharmacists, the usual chain of control for the medications doled out in hospitals world-wide, are, after all, human and to err is human. They weren't ready for the alarming results. For

Trivia Buster

6

Answers

KEEP TRACK OF YOUR TOTAL SCORE.
SEE WHERE YOU'D END UP IN THE
X-FILEAN WORLD OF HIERARCHIES,
SHADOW GOVERNMENTS,
AND CONSPIRACIES.

ONE POINTERS:

1. A pentagram.

2. His nose.

3. Leeches.

4. Sominol.

5. Abdominal liposuction.

TWO POINTERS:

6. $4000 US.

7. A broom.

8. "Vanitas Vanitatum."

9. October 31st.

10. Los Angeles.

YOUR SCORE: _____

every thousand patients who received in-hospital prescriptions in a major Boston-area hospital, some thirty-seven were *adversely* affected! And we aren't talking about trouble getting down tablets without a glass of water . . . "Adverse" reactions included serious drug interactions caused by multitudes of prescribing physicians who didn't bother to read one another's orders on the patient chart, the prescription of drugs to which the patient's file indicated they would have serious allergic reactions, and the unobserved ingestion of drugs to which the patient had not been previously exposed at all. During some six month periods of the study, the death rate directly attributable to prescription error rose as high as six for every thousand patients admitted.

The chilling reality is that stupid errors happen every day, and almost anyone working in a hospital is a source of risk to the patient. In South Africa, staff were beginning to think they had some malign presence lurking in the corner of one ward. Regardless of the condition of patients assigned to one of the ward's intensive care beds, no one ever seemed to leave it alive. The fact that the deaths occurred with clock-like regularity every Friday morning only encouraged the wild speculation working its way through the entire facility. Though the answer turned out to be all too prosaic, a member of the janitorial staff had simply been unplugging respirator plugs to accommodate her noisy floor cleaner, it also proved how precarious our hold of life can be once we allow ourselves to become vulnerable through treatments or surgeries.

Still, luckily or unluckily, depending on your point of view, most medical errors come from active attempts to alter our present condition, not from careless cleaning staffs. While it's doubtful anyone else will die in the South African intensive care ward, the remainder of the world's patients are still playing the same lottery – and the chances are often less than 50-50!

Wonder how long he's
been looking at that nose?

Take Rajeswari Ayyappan as an example. He checked into the Sloan-Kettering Cancer Center for treatment of a brain tumor. Through simple oversight, a failure to check twice before drilling, Mr. Ayyappan received his surgical treatment to the wrong side of his brain! Danny Llewellyn, a diabetic with impaired circulation, was rushed to hospital for the immediate removal of a gangrenous leg, only to lose his healthy limb instead. Jennifer Cowling awoke from her surgery to realize her surgeon had left her with a breast full of mastizing tumors and removed the perfectly healthy one. And consider the dilemma facing Tim Slaughter who received a kidney transplant only to discover the kidney he'd been given was cancerous, a situation that escaped the notice of the donor's doctor in Ohio and the United Network of Organ Sharing! A few screws assured that no more plugs could be accidentally removed from their sockets, but what's to prevent more human errors like these? Not a whole lot. Bath's Dr. Arum Pradahenda had removed six perfectly healthy limbs in a single year, all by accident, before his medical board thought it necessary to revoke his license.

X *The X-Files* crew loves to include allusions to classic literature and film and even a gore-fest like "Sanguinarium" is no exception. "Vanitas Vanitatum" is perhaps best known for its use in William Makepeace Thackeray's *Vanity Fair* and Alexandre Dumas's *The Three Musketeers*, but the original quotation is a Biblical passage from Ecclesiastes. "Vanity of vanities, saith the Preacher, vanity of vanities, all is vanity." (Ecclesiastes 1:2, King James Version) What is unusual is that, this time, when the crew included their Biblical reference, they seem to have done it without recognizing that the phrase had nothing to do with "vanity" as it's used in modern language. Maybe the New Jerusalem Bible would have given them a better understanding."Sheer futility, Qoheleth says. Sheer futility: everything is futile!" (Ecclesiastes 1:2, The New Jerusalem Bible). Taken in the context a Greek or Latin speaker would have meant and understood it, the quote falls rather flat.

X BLOOPERS!

"Sanguinarium" is one of those rare X-Filean episodes during which the audience should repeat, mantra-like, to itself that "This is only a TV show . . . This is just TV" rather than try to enumerate the number of background bloopers that worked their way into this hospital setting. Bad enough that instruments used for proctology procedures kept turning up in their plastic surgery unit, but, regardless of the discipline being practised, the good Dr. Shannon was operating in the twentieth century, shouldn't she have remembered to change clothes between patients!?

Ludicrous as it may seem, the public is now taking comfort in the fact that, since 1980, nearly twice as many physicians per year have had their license to practice on humans rescinded. And even that may not be enough if further events at Betsy Lehman's clinic are any indication. Despite Ms. Lehman's tragic death, and a tightening of the entire dosage system, a second woman undertaking the four-day treatment also received the entire amount in a single dose and was lucky to survive.

Nor are prescription errors and surgical foul-ups the only cause for concern. Another reputable study, undertaken by the Centers for Disease Control and Prevention, indicates that six to ten percent of patients entering hospitals will acquire a nosocomial infection, an infection that has nothing to do with the condition that sent them to hospital in the first place. Of those six to ten percent infected, some 80,000 will die each year. The cause? According to the study, lack of proper hygiene. And if you think that a simple switch of gloves is all that's required, think again. In January of 1997, the Associated Press ran an article that sent shivers up the back of anyone contemplating arthroscopic knee surgery. Instead of disposing of the blades used to conduct that particular type of procedure, dozens of major American hospitals were attempting to sterilize and *reuse* blades the company had clearly indicated were *one-use, disposable* items. On examination of the recycled equipment, it was discovered that bits of tissue belonging to the first patient still clung to the knives when they were used on the second! Contemplating what went into the body of third and subsequent patients is even more disgusting than a second viewing of the admittedly high-gore "Sanguinarium."

Patients looking into joint replacement have their own special concerns. Nowhere in the world are there currently regulations which prohibit the reuse of "salvaged" mechanical joints. Imagine Carrol Myers' surprise when, just two months after a hip replacement, after she found herself right back in hospital with overwhelming pain, she discovered the model she'd been given already had racked up considerable mileage in *two* other people. Neither the raging bone infection spreading through her pelvis nor the agony of having the faulty equipment removed would have been necessary if she'd received the brand-new, out-of-the-box, hip she'd been led to believe would be used.

Obviously, in an industry where a simple round-headed screw which is used to anchor a piece of broken bone and is

NOTEBOOK

Guest Filmography: O-Lan Jones

Mars Attacks! (1996) – Sue Ann Norris

The Favor (1994) – Mrs. Moyer

Natural Born Killers (1994) – Mabel

"Harts of the West" (1993) – Rose

Shelf Life (1993) – Tina

Beethoven (1992) – Biker Woman

"Danielle Steel's 'Secrets'" (1992) – Darlene Hooper

Wedlock (1991) – Saleswoman

Edward Scissorhands (1990) – Esmerelda

Martians Go Home (1990) – Stupid Medley Martian

Pacific Heights (1990) – Maid

"Seinfeld" [The Bubble Boy] (1990) – Waitress

"Lonesome Dove" (1989) – Sally Skull

"How I Got Into College" (1989) – Sally

Miracle Mile (1989) – Waitress

Married to the Mob (1988) – Phyllis

Wildfire (1988) – Mrs. Johnson

Convicted: A Mother's Story (1987) – Rhonda

X CATCH IT? Considering Mulder's apparent savvy for things pagan in "Die Hand Der Verletzt," his botched pronunciation of Samhain (SAHM-hain instead of SOW-wen or its variant SAV-en) paints him as something of a dabbler in this episode.

X CATCH IT? Dr. Franklyn, the surgeon with a penchant for other people's faces, lived at 1953 Gardner St., a particularly fitting address for a practitioner of ritual magic. Gerald Gardner was one of the men who basically re-wrote and re-invented the practise of witchcraft in Great Britain which, in turn, forms much of the art as depicted in the United States. His books were first published in 1953 when British law set aside prohibitions against witchcraft.

CASE CREDITS

WRITTEN BY: Vivian Mayhew and
    Valerie Mayhew
DIRECTED BY: Kim Manners
ORIGINAL PRODUCTION
    NUMBER: 4X06
ORIGINAL US AIR DATE: 11/10/96

GUEST CAST

DR. HARRISON LLOYD
    John Juliani
DR. THERESA SHANNON
    Arlene Mazerolle
DR. JACK FRANKLIN
    Richard Beymer
DR. PRABU AMANPOUR
    Paul Raskin
DR. MITCHELL KAPLAN
    Gregory Thirloway
DR. HARTMAN
    Martin Evans
DR. SALLY SANFORD
    Marie Stillin
NURSE REBECCA WAITE
    O-lan Jones
LIPOSUCTION PATIENT
    Nancy J. Lilley
SKIN PEEL PATIENT
    Celine Lockhart
JILL HOLWAGERM
    Nina Roman
ATTORNEY
    Andrew Arlie

DEATH TOLL

1 MAN: 1 stabbed to death during
    surgery
4 WOMEN: 1 eaten by acid, 1 "laser-ed"
    to death, 1 bled to death as a result
    of pins in the digestive track, and
    1 died off-screen
5 PRIOR VICTIMS: 1 male – suicide
    by overdose, 4 unknown – medical
    error

not all that different from the ones found in big boxes in the local garden shop sells for $75 US *each*, cost cutting is a major problem. It's the obvious reason behind the reuse of disposable equipment, the recycling of medical products and the short post-operative stays. However, it's not just emergency patients and managed health care units that are trying to save a dollar. In times of recession, even the traditionally up-market services, like plastic and aesthetic surgical units, are trying to keep costs down.

That appears to be what happened when two Californian doctors offered to do a "bulk order" for one of their female patients. In exchange for $20,000, Judy Fernandez was to undergo a literal marathon of treatment that included a mini-facial, liposuctioning twenty pounds of fat from six different locations, reinserting some fat into legs and buttocks for "bodysculpting," laser skin resurfacing, and an eyebrow lift. The myriad of procedures were to be completed in one eleven-hour session because it was a "package deal" that would have cost much more if undertaken in the usual fashion as a number of shorter surgeries. Instead of coming out with a renewed body, the woman from La Hambra apparently bled to death on the operating table. Though evidence is still being gathered, it appears the cut-rate price didn't include little frills like having typed blood on hand throughout the procedure.

Imagine the pressure that could be brought to bear on an Aesthetic Surgery Unit which was *expected* to deliver up to seventy per cent of a hospital's operating costs.

Perhaps the "new" math has clouded the fiscal issues at work in hospitals, or perhaps my grandfather simply had more common sense to begin with, but for him the equation has always been simple. Too many patients plus not enough staff plus too many bean counters equals too many mistakes. As three major studies in 1997 alone have just confirmed, however, he was probably right all along.

"Musings of a Cigarette-Smoking Man"

Case: XF-4X07-11-17-96

CASE SUMMARY

The Lone Gunmen are in a panic, afraid for their own lives, when they believe they've stumbled onto the clue which could lead Mulder to the truth behind the Cigarette-Smoking Man's deep cover. Is he a monster? A product of his times? An object of pity?

CASE HISTORY
Through the Smoke, Darkly

It's unusual for a "bad guy" to attract a strong fan following – especially a character whose redeeming qualities lurk only in the vivid imaginations of a trio of paranoid, borderline schizophrenics with a taste for cheese steaks. Yet, despite portraying "the most hated man since JR," that's exactly what's happening for William B. Davis!

Perhaps it's the smile that startles those who are lucky enough to meet him "out of character," or the genuine pleasure he exudes when meeting fans, or even the unconscious habit of waving away any stray bits of smoke that drift his way. Whichever, it doesn't take long to realize just how good an actor Davis is when the character he's created can so perfectly hide the charming man behind all that smoke.

When Davis took on the role of the Cigarette-Smoking Man, there was, literally, no back story for him to absorb. The man was as much a mystery to the actor who'd bring him to life as he was to a curious Scully in that premiere scene or to the audience who'd spend the next four years watching his every blink and glance, searching for some nuance of meaning. In one sense, it's every actor's dream to be given a compelling character guaranteed to capture attention every time he steps into a scene. On a day to day basis, however, it's often difficult for actors to relate to characters with so little definition and Davis wouldn't be much of an actor if he hadn't been building his own little world for the Cigarette-Smoking Man.

Though some will find it surprising, Davis chooses to see his dark alter ego as a hero. Like the character of Skinner, whom everyone has chosen to perceive as one of the "good guys," CSM is a character caught between powerful forces. The Consortium to which he must report, the sources and operatives for whose conduct he is ultimately responsible and the civilians he must work amongst seem little different than the hierarchy of authority and responsibility to which Skinner and the others are answerable. Like Mulder, The Cigarette-Smoking Man has a goal, a plan, a future he believes in desperately. As he told Mulder, his position has few perks. He has no home, no family, none of the things that "normal" people take for granted. Implicit in his speech is a comparison between the two men, two men who are, apparently, equally willing to sacrifice their chance at normalcy for something they clearly believe is more important. And, like Scully, he doesn't back away from truths, even unpleasant ones. He never denies anyone's opinion of him, never justifies his actions. In some characters, those same qualities could be signs of strength. Perhaps there's some logic in Davis's choice, a choice that, even if wrong, certainly adds several layers of dimension to what could, just as easily, degenerate into some cardboard cutout bad guy.

Even if he's wrong, if The Cigarette-Smoking Man turns out to be as despicable as most X-Philes anticipate, his fans can rejoice in the knowledge that, tied as closely to the mythology episodes as he is, they'll be seeing lots more of his scheming yet.

FACTS

● William B. Davis is a past Canadian National Waterskiing Champion who doesn't do too badly on snow either.

● Not only is he a nonsmoker who suffers through those smoking scenes by dragging back on Honey Rose herbal cigarettes that smell even worse than the real thing, he's a

7

THESE ARE THE EASY ONES! TAKE A SINGLE POINT FOR EACH CORRECT ANSWER.

1. What is written on The Cigarette-Smoking Man's lighter?

2. How does Mulder describe Frohike?

3. By what first name did The Cigarette-Smoking Man call Deep Throat?

4. What *nom de plume* did The Cigarette-Smoking Man employ?

5. What Olympic event did The Cigarette-Smoking Man claim to have rigged?

THESE WILL MAKE YOU THINK, SO GIVE YOURSELF TWO POINTS FOR A CORRECT RESPONSE.

6. What piece of equipment does Frohike declare a "piece of crap"?

7. What newsletter do the Lone Gunmen publish?

8. How did The Cigarette-Smoking Man's father supposedly die?

9. How much did The Cigarette-Smoking Man pay for his movie?

10. Which classical poet could The Cigarette-Smoking Man quote?

Answers

KEEP TRACK OF YOUR TOTAL SCORE.
SEE WHERE YOU'D END UP IN THE
X-FILEAN WORLD OF HIERARCHIES,
SHADOW GOVERNMENTS,
AND CONSPIRACIES.

ONE POINTERS:

1. "TRUST NO ONE"

2. A "little puppy dog."

3. Ronald.

4. Raul Bloodworth.

5. Hockey in 1980.

TWO POINTERS:

6. The CPM-700.

7. *The Magic Bullet.*

8. In a Louisiana electric chair,
for treason.

9. 90 cents.

10. Aeschylus.

YOUR SCORE _____

reformed nonsmoker who is known to ask perfect strangers to put out their smokes.

● Davis not only acts, he teaches acting at his own school in Vancouver.

● Off-screen, Mitch Pileggi calls The Cigarette-Smoking Man "Cigarette Butt."

Filmography

Unforgettable (1996) – Doctor

"The Outer Limits" [Out of Body] (1996) – John Wymer

"Sliders" [Eggheads] (1996) – Prof. Myman

"Unknown Circumstances" (1995)

Dangerous Intentions (1995) – Group Leader

"The Outer Limits" [Conversion] (1995) – Ed

"Don't Talk to Strangers" (1994) – Huddleston

"Heart of a Child" (1994) – Vern

"Diagnosis of Murder" (1992) – Marvin Parkins

"Anything to Survive" (1990) – Dr. Reynolds

"It" (1990) – Mr. Gedreau

Look Who's Talking (1989) – Drug Doctor

"Midnight Matinee" (1988) – Heath Harris

Head Office (1986) – University Dean

"The Cuckoo Bird" (1985) – Ted

The Dead Zone (1983) – Ambulance Driver

Appearances on The X-Files:

Season One	Season Two	Season Three	Season Four
"The X-Files"	*"Little Green Men"*	*"The Blessing Way"*	*"Herrenvolk"*
"Young At Heart" (CIA Agent)	*"Sleepless"*	*"Paper Clip"*	*"Musings of a Cigarette-Smoking Man"*
"Tooms"	*"Ascension"*	*"731"*	
"The Erlenmeyer Flask"	*"One Breath"*	*"Apocrypha"*	*"Tunguska"*
	"F. Emasculata"	*"Avatar"*	*"Terma"*
	"Anasazi"	*"Wetwired"*	*"Memento Mori"*
		"Talitha Cumi"	*"Zero Sum"*
			"Gethsemane"

Just how many cigarettes has The Cigarette-Smoking Man lit over four years? Good thing for William B. Davis, a reformed non-smoker, that they're all clove cigarettes.

CASE NOTES
That Certain Touch

Some painters have styles so individual you can pick out their work anywhere, even across a room at an opening full of clinking glasses, falsetto laughter, bad hats and worse lighting. If Jim Wong and Glen Morgan were artists, they'd probably need a gallery all their own just to contain the many styles and formats with which they've been known to experiment. Even with the writing team split into writer and director, something almost tangible marks it as theirs. Comparing "Beyond the Sea" to this season's "Home" easily highlights the differing moods they can evoke. "Ice" and "The Field Where I Died," while equally

CATCH IT? Yet another "10-13" reference! This time it's hiding as a United Nations Security Council Resolution which states: "Any country capturing such an entity is responsible for its immediate extermination."

An unlikely – and adorable – trio of spies. Could these three have possibly penetrated The Cigarette-Smoking Man's deepest cover? Nah.

Ⓧ CATCH IT? Yet another of the Morgan and Wong signatures, CSM is reading *The Manchurian Candidate*.

dramatic, draw on two different traditions for their overall effect. "Ice" is among the best of the suspense-styled dramas, the kind that moves at a hectic clip without becoming a simple action script sacrificing all the power of clearly drawn characters for a few explosions. "The Field Where I Died" tuned down the action to let suspense arise from the characters themselves; the action was internal instead of external.

Still, though their episodes all explore different aspects of scriptwriting and story-telling, there are signature details throughout "Musings of a Cigarette-Smoking Man" to make it as uniquely theirs as any of their other scripts.

First, and always, there's the humour. In "Ice," the jokes were "bathroom" and broad; cracks about not judging a naked man by how he looked "in the Arctic" were classics. "Squeeze" mixed its humor with a high "ewwww!" factor to deliver lines like "Is there any way I can get it off my fingers quickly – without betraying my cool exterior?" as Mulder watched bile drip from his fingertips, a trend that continued unbroken in "Tooms." Even in "Musings of a Cigarette-Smoking Man," an episode so tied up in itself that there hardly seemed room for the witticisms Morgan and Wong integrated so smoothly into their other work, there was room for a twist or two. Putting Saddam Hussein on hold? And how about them Bills? Actually, that fulfilled two of the points on a Morgan–Wong script, humor and a gratuitous sports reference!

Having Morgan Weisser appear in the episode followed yet another of their post-*Space: Above and Beyond* traditions, namely including members of their own show in any episode of *The*

Despite having less than an hour of total air time over four seasons, The Lone Gunmen remain perennial fan favourites.

ASE CREDITS

WRITTEN BY: Glen Morgan and
   James Wong
DIRECTED BY: Rob Bowman
ORIGINAL PRODUCTION
   NUMBER: 4X07
ORIGINAL US AIR DATE: 11/17/96

GUEST CAST

THE CIGARETTE-SMOKING MAN
   William B. Davis
DEEP THROAT
   Jerry Hardin
YOUNG CIGARETTE-SMOKING MAN
   Chris Owens
YOUNG BILL MULDER
   Dean Aylesworth
DIRECTOR
   David Fredericks
YERS
   Bruce Harwood
FROHIKE
   Tom Braidwood
GENERAL FRANCIS
   Donnelly Rhodes
CORPORAL
   Anthony Ashbee
TROOP LEADER
   Colin Lawrence
MAJOR GENERAL
   Michael St. John Smith
IDE
   Peter Hanlon
LEE HARVEY OSWALD
   Morgan Weisser
JAMES EARL RAY
   Paul Jarrett
DON
   Laurie Murdoch
MATLOCK
   Marc Baur
ONES
   Jude Zachary
OB MAN
   Peter Mele
GENT
   Dan Zukovic
CUBAN MAN
   Gonzalo Canton
SUPERVISOR
   Steve Oatway

DEATH TOLL

MEN: shot to death.
ALIEN: gender unknown shot to
   death

X-Files they could! Considering the sterling performance turned in by the S:AAB performers in not only "Musings of a Cigarette-Smoking Man" but "Never Again" and "The Field Where I Died," however, it's doubtful too many X-Philes were complaining about the obvious casting bias.

X-Philes were delighted to have the talented writing team back again, saddened to see them go again, and are now looking forward to see what new original work they're going to pull out of their pocket.

X-FILES Episodes Written by James Wong and/or Glen Morgan

"Squeeze"

"Shadows"

"Ice"

"Beyond the Sea"

"E.B.E."

"Tooms"

"Little Green Men"

"Blood"

"3"

"One Breath"

"Die Hand Der Verletzt"

"Home"

"The Field Where I Died"

"Musings of a Cigarette-Smoking Man"

"Never Again"

CODE NAME:

"Paper Hearts"

Case: XF-4X08-12-15-96

CASE SUMMARY

Mulder's personal ghosts are rising from the graves of sixteen murdered children as a killer, whose chosen victimology could, all too easily, include Samantha Mulder, decides to play with his captor's mind. Rocked by the killer's claims, his intimate knowledge of details only a young Fox should know, Mulder begins doubting himself, his memories, and his beliefs. It's Scully, immune to the charm the killer turned on his victims and their families, who must help Mulder "dig up" this particular truth – while attempting to keep his career intact and Mulder himself on the right side of the law.

CASE HISTORY:
Fiction imitating art imitating life

Unless the audience watching "Paper Hearts" included an unusually high proportion of Literature majors, they were probably left wondering what possible connection there could be between this week's Bad Guy and Lewis Carroll, the creator of a host of fantastic tales and creatures that have entertained children for more than a hundred years. However, for those with an interest in the author, as well as his writing, the addition of the Carrollian allusions added another, subtle, layer of enjoyment to an already outstanding episode. For this portion of the audience, it was really no surprise that character John Lee Roche identified so closely with Lewis Carroll, aka Charles Lutwidge Dodgson, or that he became so enamoured of his best-known work, *Alice's Adventures in Wonderland*. After all, if even a fraction of what has been written about Charles Dodgson is true, and if our understanding of paedophiles is even semi-accurate, the fictional Roche and Carroll share one overwhelming passion, a "fondness" for young girls. Though a centenary book on Dodgson's life speculates that he was involved in an adulterous affair with his boss's wife, Lorina Liddell, most literary biographers believe it was the boss's ten-year-old daughter, Alice Liddell, later to become immortalized as the Alice of

EYEWITNESS STATEMENT

"November 27th, 1973. I watched the house for hours. I parked across the way, out over there. I was just casing. I wasn't planning for this to be the night. But then, all of a sudden, your parents leave and I figure...."

John Lee Roche

Wonderland, who was the object of Dodgson's sexual interest!

Certainly, almost any modern-day criminal profiler would find Dodgson's pattern of behavior, his personal history, interesting, even alarming.

Early in life, Dodgson turned to fantasy to entertain himself and his ten siblings. He produced stories, poetry, "newsletters," and illustrations. At fourteen, when most young men's thoughts are occupied with fourteen-year-old girls, Dodgson busied himself with self-made issues of "Useful and Instructive Poetry." Instead of the more mature female figures scrawled in the back of his classmates' books, young Charles was writing nonsense poems and children's stories. While no one seems to seriously suggest the Dodgson children were abused, sexually or otherwise, it's also interesting to note that *all eleven children* suffered from speech impediments, a condition often found among abuse victims. His stutter apparently contributed to his discomfort in the social company of adults and, long after his contemporaries began preferring adult conversation, Charles Dodgson seemed most at ease with pre-pubescent children. In the presence of young girls, his stammer all but disappeared! Modern psychologists wouldn't create personality sketches based on any single trait, but would certainly agree that his comfort/confidence level and the severity of his stammer were related.

His interest in young girls, reflected in the numerous sketches and more formal drawings he composed of them, would last throughout his lifetime, but, in 1855, Charles Dodgson was introduced to both Alice Liddell and that new-fangled marvel, the camera. He continued to photograph other girls, but, if sheer number of photographs is any indication, it was Alice Liddell who caught and held his imagination. Nor were all his photographs and pictures what one might expect from Victorian England. For reasons modern parents would find difficult to understand, many of these girls' parents happily allowed Dodgson to draw and photograph their children in

8

THESE ARE THE EASY ONES!
TAKE A SINGLE POINT FOR
EACH CORRECT ANSWER.

1. How many victims did John Lee Roche originally admit to murdering?

2. What was embroidered on Addie's jumper pocket?

3. Roche drove an unusual model of car. What?

4. In what book did Mulder find the hearts?

5. Which model vacuum cleaner did Bill Mulder purchase?

THESE WILL MAKE YOU THINK,
SO GIVE YOURSELF TWO POINTS
FOR A CORRECT RESPONSE.

6. How did Samantha break her collar bone?

7. Name the child Roche met on the plane.

8. What airline did Mulder and Roche take?

9. How far is it from West Tisbury to Chilmark?

10. What street did Roche live on in Boston?

Trivia Buster

8

Answers

KEEP TRACK OF YOUR TOTAL SCORE. SEE WHERE YOU'D END UP IN THE X-FILEAN WORLD OF HIERARCHIES, SHADOW GOVERNMENTS, AND CONSPIRACIES.

ONE POINTERS:

1. Thirteen. Roche thought it sounded "magical."

2. A dollar sign, to remind the tooth fairy to leave a present.

3. An El Camino.

4. *Alice in Wonderland*.

5. The ElectroVac Princess.

TWO POINTERS:

6. She fell from a swing.

7. Caitlin.

8. Seaboard Air.

9. Six miles.

10. Alice.

YOUR SCORE _____

states of complete undress! It's difficult for us to imagine how Dodgson phrased such requests, much less why the parents allowed him to stare at their nude children for hours on end. Some psychologists and criminal investigators, however, think there are current parallels. They point to "Little Miss" beauty pageants, modern advertising schemes, and even sports like gymnastics. Each of those situations forces young children to appear more mature than they are, and allows adults access to the children in exchange for the perceived fame the activity will bring, and forces the child to appear scantily or provocatively clad. In any case, Dodgson would soon amass photo albums to rival those of paedophiles more than a century later.

The camera also allowed him to indulge his flights of fantasy once again. While he did a considerable amount of "normal" portraiture, he also dabbled in "staged" scenarios. In one famous picture, Alice Liddell appears in a Little Red Riding Hood costume. Similar fantasy poses are frequently found among the paedophile's photographic library.

Despite Dodgson's apparent acceptance into polite society, things may not have been quite as innocent and tranquil as most of Carroll's fans would like to believe. Though he was permitted access to these young girls, he was also frequently cut off without any explanation that has survived to the present time. His family never tried to suppress any of his illustrations, yet one of his heirs excised those sections of Dodgson's diaries that dealt with his sudden exclusion, by Mrs. Liddell, from the company of her three daughters, including Alice. In fact, it was while *Alice's Adventures in Wonderland* was being illustrated and published that Dodgson was completely excluded from the Liddell home. If not for the fact that the girls' governess was their sole guardian during their parent's summer vacation, and that the governess didn't enforce the ban on Dodgson, he might never have seen Alice Liddell again, never taken the girls on boat trips along the Thames, and never written *Alice's Adventures in Wonderland*.

Later, Dodgson himself seemed to lose interest in young Alice, perhaps not coincidentally, when she passed through puberty and took on the physical attributes of a mature woman.

Like Roche, who could recall the minute details of his former "glory," and preferred to indulge those reminiscences while fingering his souvenir "paper hearts," Dodgson would also relive his days with Alice through his pictures and an astonishingly detailed memory. Years later, he would commit those memories to paper as words as well as illustrations:

> *"Full many a year has slipped away, since that 'golden afternoon' that gave thee [the Alice stories] birth, but I can call it up as clearly as if it were yesterday – the cloudless blue above, the watery mirror below, the boat drifting idly on its way, the tinkle of the drops that fell from the oars, as they waved so sleepily to and fro, and (the one bright gleam of life in all the slumberous scene) the three eager young faces, hungry for news of fairy-land . . ."*

Roche's attention to details like the "green rancher" with its "beds of mint" carries the same tone of fantastic perfection that flows through most of Dodgson's descriptions of his time with the young girls of his acquaintance. While Mulder knew what was hidden behind Roche's idyllic memories, we may never know what, if anything more than latent paedophilia, was hidden behind Dodgson's.

Comparing Dodgson to real-life descriptions of serial child molesters is an eerie experience. From a variety of reports and formal profiles, it's easy to draw lines of similarity between the real, the suspected, and the well-researched fictional personalities linked by "Paper Hearts."

". . . white male in his thirties . . ." Like the majority of real world paedophiles, both Roche and Dodgson began acting out their fantasies just after turning thirty.

". . . a 'man-next-door,' respectable in appearance, non-threatening . . ." In today's culture, the door-to-door salesman is a rather pathetic, if respectable, figure. Dodgson, the stuttering mathematician, probably presented an equally unthreatening picture.

". . . will have a job that allows access to private homes and children . . ." Roche acknowledged that vacuum sales weren't his life, but, as he told Mulder, they allowed him to get "inside," where he could observe his victims and familiarize himself with the layout of his next crime scene. Dodgson's portrait work, completely legitimate and of a high enough quality to be displayed in dozens of reputable galleries, allowed him hours of access over a considerable length of time.

". . . likely to have been associated with previous, if nebulous, accusations of inappropriate sexual behavior towards children . . ." Dodgson's on-again-off-again relationship with his "young friend's" parents would likely have been a key factor in any court case had Dodgson crossed the line he apparently imposed on his activities.

". . . have some connection to photography . . ." Dodgson's was obvious, but Roche's choice of souvenir, the cloth hearts, was equally intimate and certainly served the same purpose. Statistically, upwards of ninety percent of paedophiles maintain some sort of collection.

". . . likely to participate in childish activities . . ." Roche played "games" with Mulder's head; Dodgson held tea parties for his young friends and spent most of his life creating stories and poems to entertain them.

The conspicuous, and important, difference between Roche and his literary idol is that Dodgson certainly didn't kill – likely never actually even touched – the objects of his desire. Whether it's because the general public can actually find even a paedophile's "thwarted love" romantic, or because Dodgson actively decided not to carry his fantasies farther than the page, there's no indication that his sexual interest in children was ever consummated. Dodgson, poet, mathematician, artist and minister, would likely be appalled to think of his Alice tales being the preferred reading of a character like Roche.

CASE NOTES
Those Niggling Little Legalities . . .

Fortunately, Special Agent Fox Mulder will never be assigned any real life cases. While his antics make for entertaining, and often amusing, television, it's unlikely we'd want such a "loose cannon" working for, or against, us. In this one episode, he managed to bend, if not break, nearly every conceivable guideline handed out to raw recruits – and that's only when he wasn't busy breaking the law!

Not once, but twice, he mucked about in a crime scene, contaminating the area for the forensics team at the first location and dragging his partner into questionable activities at the second. Perhaps, if Mulder actually managed to get the odd suspect into a courtroom, he'd remember how critical the collection of evidence and the chain of custody are. And, once inside a courtroom, he'd probably also be reminded that another name for "detailing" an El Camino without it's owner's foreknowledge is "destruction of private property."

And determining just how many laws and/or principles of ethical conduct were broken between Mulder's first interview with Roche, where he assaulted an inmate in federal custody, and his last, where he finally shot his nemesis, might take a team of Department of Justice lawyers several months to sort out! The only absolute certainty? The employment status of *former* Special Agent Fox Mulder.

While the confirmed X-Phile is expected to be sympathetic to the overwhelming angst suffered by their Hero, to excuse his forays into quasi-illegal situations as the means to a higher end, new fans tuning in for their first season could be excused for wondering just who the good guys are. Haven't The Cigarette-Smoking Man, The Well-Manicured Man, X, and even Deep Throat all spent on-screen time pondering the question of whether their ends justified the means they'd used, the sacrifices they'd made along the way?

Nor are Mulder's "questionable" activities reserved for those

X It's no surprise that Mulder is constantly sinking hoops. David Duchovny is an accomplished athlete, though he gave up dreams of a basketball career when he stopped growing at a measly six feet.

CASE CREDITS

WRITTEN BY: Vince Gilligan
DIRECTED BY: Rob Bowman
ORIGINAL PRODUCTION
     NUMBER: 4X08
ORIGINAL US AIRDATE: 12/15/96

GUEST CAST

LOCAL COP
     Paul Bittante
LOCAL AGENT
     John Dadey
CAITLIN ROSS
     Carly McKillip
SAMANTHA MULDER
     Vanessa Morley
JOHN LEE ROCHE
     Tom Noonan
YOUNG MOTHER
     Sonia Norris
ASSISTANT DIRECTOR WALTER
S. SKINNER
     Mitch Pileggi
ROBERT SPARKS
     Byrne Piven
MRS. MULDER
     Rebecca Toolan

instances that involve his missing sister! Samantha was nowhere to be seen when he pulled the Peeping Tom routine in "3." She certainly wasn't a factor in "War of the Coprophages" when he decided to try breaking and entering a federal installation. Or, for that matter, when he unilaterally allowed a murderer to walk off into the sunset in "Firewalker." No, his latitude with things legal pops up on an almost weekly basis.

Unfortunately, the ability of one character to do practically whatever he chooses has a marked, and not propitious, effect on surrounding characters. Scully and Skinner, characters built around a rock-solid sense of justice, become less and less credible as writers force those characters to accept, if not endorse, Mulder's activities. That basic conflict results in scenes like the one in Skinner's office where Scully, who spends most of the rest of the episode telling Mulder he's too close, can suddenly find a half dozen reasons to keep Mulder *on* the case!

It's hard not to wonder just where Mulder himself draws the line.

Guest Filmography: Tom Noonan

With over twenty years in the business, you'd expect Tom Noonan, given an intriguing character like Roche, to turn in a stunning performance – and he did. If you'd like to catch some of his other, equally inspired, performances, try catching one of these:

Heat (1995)

The Wife (1995) (also directed)

North and South III (1994)

What Happened Was . . . (1994) (also wrote and directed)

Last Action Hero (1993)

Robocop II (1990)

Collision Course (1989) (portrayed character named Scully!)

The Monster Squad (1987)

Manhunter (1986)

The Man With One Red Shoe (1986)

Heaven's Gate (1980)

CODE NAME:

"Tunguska"

Case: XF-4X09-11-24-96

CASE SUMMARY

When Mulder decides to backtrack the trail of a diplomatic pouch containing a rock with some rather unusual properties, including a knack for being in the vicinity of people who die unexpectedly, he leaves Scully holding a different sort of bag in front of a Senate investigating committee. Her position, along with Assistant Director Skinner's, gets increasingly uncomfortable as it becomes obvious that Mulder prefers roaming about the Russian countryside to accepting his own Senate invitation. Mulder quickly discovers, however, that foreign governments aren't one bit more amenable to his snooping when his poking lands him in a forced labor camp.

CASE HISTORY
When the sky really is falling!

On June 30, 1908 seismic shock waves set the needles of earthquake recorders dancing all over Russia and jostled instruments as far away as the American capital of Washington, D.C. Closer to the source, a swampy area between the Upper, Lower and Stony Tungus Rivers, naked-eye watchers stared upward at the mushroom cloud blacking out the sun all that day, which, for the next several nights, reflected so much of the setting sun's light that Siberians two hundred miles away could read their paper without any need for lamps. The "black rain" that fell for the next week kept people eyeing the sky warily even after the odd glow faded. Even closer, Tungus tribesmen, some of whom claimed to see a streak of light flash across the sky earlier that night, were knocked from their feet by the hot shock waves.

Anyone closer than that simply didn't survive the blast that burnt acres of forest, snapped two-foot thick trees like matchsticks, and flattened a further *800 square miles* of tough, coniferous forest. Whole herds of reindeer died in an instant; those that survived were frequently found to be susceptible to a "scabby disease" previously unknown to local residents.

EYEWITNESS STATEMENT

"Agents Mulder and Scully intercepted a diplomatic pouch here in Washington last night. I'm afraid it's created a problem in foreign policy circles. Quite a problem actually."

Cigarette-Smoking Man

It would be some twenty years, however, before a Russian scientist, Leonid Kulik, came, saw, and was overawed by the devastation. Trees, laid out in rows neat enough to be the envy of any honour guard, marched across the hillsides for as far as the eye could see. In less than five minutes a blast, with a force some estimate as equal to a thousand of the bomb dropped on Hiroshima, had utterly levelled an area larger than London and New York City combined, an area as big as ten of Mulder's beloved Martha's Vineyard. And no one really knew why.

An American, gazing out over the ranks of trees, especially after hearing of the black clouds, the glowing skies, and the rumbling roar that accompanied the Tunguska Event, could easily believe they were looking at the results of a massive volcanic eruption. Televised images of the area around Mount St. Helens, with its ashen landscapes of toppled trees radiating out from what remained of the cone, certainly bore a strong resemblance to what this site might have looked like immediately after the Tunguska blast. In fact, a volcanic explosion was one of the early theories before Kulik arrived. After all, the Krakatoa eruption, a comparatively recent event, happening only twenty-five years earlier in 1883, had thrown dust over thirty miles in the air, debris that would fall again over a ten-day period as much as 3,000 miles away. The Krakatoa blast was clearly heard as far as 2,500 miles away and the glow from its dust cloud lasted even longer than that of the Tunguska Event.

The theory quickly lost favor when no cone, or evidence of volcanic ash and debris, could be found in the relatively flat, swampy region. And, although Tunguska isn't a bustling metropolis, the area was lightly inhabited and there were no witnesses to any of the aftershocks that normally follow even the less massive quakes.

Kulik, however, was a geologist with an interest in meteorites, not volcanoes, and he'd been collecting fragments at impact sites for some years before he finally made it to

Trivia Buster

9

THESE ARE THE EASY ONES! TAKE A SINGLE POINT FOR EACH CORRECT ANSWER.

1. What former "partner" turned up in a group of militiamen?

2. Where is Walter Skinner's new apartment located?

3. Where did Dr. Sacks think the rock originated?

4. Which agent accompanies Scully inside the isolation unit?

5. Where did Krycek spend some awkward time "hanging around"?

THESE WILL MAKE YOU THINK, SO GIVE YOURSELF TWO POINTS FOR A CORRECT RESPONSE.

6. What group did Scully have to testify in front of?

7. What company owned the truck rented to transport the explosives?

8. Which "Long Term Parking" area nearly became Krycek's home-away-from-home?

9. For what destination did Mulder procure two tickets?

10. Which airline brought the second courier to the United States?

Trivia Buster

9

Tunguska. Far from being disappointed to shelve the volcano theory, he spent the next fourteen years actively searching for evidence that might support a meteorite- or comet-impact explanation for Tunguska. Including the first expedition in 1927, Kulik led five separate expeditions to the remote region. Considering the technology available to him at the time, the inhospitability of the terrain, and the short warmer season during which scientists could work, Kulik's documentation of the scene was somewhat incredible. He photographed the area, perhaps recognizing that the natural process of reforestation would certainly hide the sight from later colleagues, and provided the first record of the extent of damage and the first rough maps. He dragged the murky swamps for evidence of fragments, a task made even more daunting by the clouds of mosquitos that could drive a man half-crazy. He collected the contradictory eyewitness testimony of locals, keeping accurate records without attempting to make their statements fit his own theories, something that would happen in later situations when other investigators arrived.

The Second World War influenced the Tunguska inquiries in two, completely unrelated, ways. As images of the explosions over Japan were flashed around the world, some few scientists quickly associated the "mushroom" clouds with the similar formations reported over Tunguska. The only problem with even the early expressions of a connection between the man-made explosions and the Tunguska Event was that, in 1908, no such technology existed! Perhaps, at a time when paranoia was running high, science-fiction literature and film were popular, and there were still no explanations for Tunguska, the notion that some "other" agency, something not terrestrial, crash-landed into, or exploded over, Tunguska might enjoy popular speculation. Combining any public audience's fascination with the fantastic and with some unusual aspect of local lore is a pretty good way to ensure people continue to toy with any given idea. A glance at any supermarket magazine rack is evidence of that. And, with as good a mystery as Tunguska, it was probably inevitable that something similar would occur with Tunguska theories.

Sometime after the Second World War, local legends of the Tungus tribesmen, whose shamans tied themselves to the ground in order to avoid being taken by "sky people" during the trance period when their spirits communed with the spirits of the sky, surfaced. These stories, much more symbolic than real to the Tungus themselves, were quickly whipped into "alien abduction" scenarios that even Mulder would consider beyond the limits of "extreme possibility." Before long, the craft that might have crashed or exploded in Tunguska became "alien space craft" and the reasons why evidence was difficult to obtain was whispered to be "government coverups" and "military intelligence." Such theories quickly became popular again after the "Roswell Incident" became readily available media fodder.

The more extravagant explanations, that Tunguska was the Russian version of Area 51, that even the Siberians mightn't be aware of a well-concealed base of alien operations, or that the aliens were already establishing a permanent underground society and that they'd chosen Tunguska because its isolation would provide them plenty of time to become a force on their new home world, did, with satisfying speed to serious researchers, fade out.

What was left, however, was the idea that, as there was no evidence to support even the least fantastic theory, that of a meteor or asteroid impact, it might be time to open up the field of inquiry to other areas. It was about this time that the "black hole" and "anti-matter" theories came into vogue. In both cases, theorists speculated that some cosmic anomaly with virtually no size had struck and, in effect, passed through the planet. These theories didn't account for the streak of light that was reported earlier, but did have the advantage of explaining the total lack of physical evidence at the site. And, as no one had ever observed, or really even speculated about, the consequences of such "impacts," there were few well-developed reasons why some unknown space particle or a tiny gravitational quirk *couldn't* be responsible.

Still, the promoters of such theories were in the minority. There had been a streak of light reported by dozens of independent observers, even if they couldn't seem to agree on the direction or altitude of the object making the display. That streak and the deafening boom that accompanied it all seemed to point to a considerably more solid culprit. To determine the angle and probably strike location, other scientists would meticulously map the area again, enlarging and expanding Kulik's early efforts by adding notations on the direction of tree fall, the degree and depth of accompanying burns, and chronicling the still-standing trees at the supposed epicenter of the blast. Kulik himself couldn't be part of these refinements. World War II's second effect on the Tunguska Event investigations had been the loss of the enthusiastic scientist who died in a prisoner of war camp far from the great mystery.

But other young Russians shared his curiosity and expeditions continued to explore the area. Foremost among the curious was mathematician Wilhelm Fast. Over a period of three decades, he and a group of zealous students finally finished the Tunguska map. They also lugged out soil and tree samples which would preserve what evidence there was and continue to spark the imaginations of yet more scientists. It was Fast's meticulous map that allowed a combination of physicists, mathematicians and geologists to determine that whatever it was that caused the razing of acres of trees, it happened about four miles up, not on the ground at all. The clues that might add up to an answer were starting to come together. The next pieces of the puzzle would come from outside the region, from scientists who, like those who longed to explore nearby Lake Baikal, had, for political reasons, remained barred from the sensitive military region.

There was Menotti Galli, who thought it was about time someone checked for the heavy isotopes and radiation so frequently associated with cosmic intruders. Even if, as was now being speculated, the meteor had been essentially vaporized higher in the atmosphere, some particle, some energetic residue, had to have been produced. After almost ninety years, however, it wasn't going to be easy to find. Repeated dragging of the deep swamps had already proven that there simply were no larger fragments to analyse. As in the beginning, the trees were the only evidence that anything had happened in Siberia, and Galli made them the focus of his investigations. All trees produce various amounts of resin, the same substance which played such a pivotal role in Michael Crichton's tales of re-engineered dinosaur DNA. Trees also provided a rough chronology of the area in which they'd grown. A tree that survived the original blast might well have been peppered with the most minute particles from the exploding meteor, particles that would be in rings of approximately ninety year's age.

In partnership with a colleague named Giuseppe Longo, Galli began a physical and chemical examination of tree samples. Early results looked positive, but, one chunk of wood, which is all they had, was hardly representative of the overall region, or the soil, water and air samples that provide baselines against which further results could be gauged. In their turn, they too would discover how miserable a Siberian swamp is when its flying insects, frantic for the blood meals necessary to reproduction, discover a couple of healthy Italian men in their midst. Having given up what was becoming known as "Tunguska's blood sacrifice," however, they returned home with more samples. Months later, as they identified oddly shaped

X Did you catch the name of the Customs officer who interrogated the first courier at the airport? "Vince" is the first name of long-time *X-Files* writer Vince Gilligan. "Mayhew" is the surname of two newcomers to the writing stable as well as the militiaman incarcerated in connection with the explosives found in the early scenes.

particles with the assistance of high-powered microscopes that Kulik would likely have drooled over, it became clear that they'd found what everyone was looking for . . . the physical result of an explosion at an altitude which would explain the lack of a central crater!

The only real remaining question is just *how* did a sizeable chunk of space rock end up as a mass of grains so tiny that more than a thousand of them, laid side by side, would barely make a line an inch long? Frankly, even with the gigantic technological leaps that have taken place since native Siberians looked up to see a light flash across the early morning sky, that's something of a mystery. Computer models suggest that an object entering the atmosphere from a steep angle may well deform sufficiently to create heat even more intense than previously suspected, converting hydrogen, creating, in effect, a naturally occurring hydrogen bomb. Other models, however, equally well-supported by current concepts of high-speed impacts, produce the classic impact-crater and "ripple-effect" zone that allowed other researchers to discover the Yucatan crash site that may have killed off the dinosaurs.

All of which leaves the lay audience with considerably more practical, and pointed, questions. What would have happened had the Tunguska Event exploded over Rome, or London, or Washington? First of all, would there have been any warning? Can modern astronomy find such small, but potentially deadly, rocks out against the vast canopy of space? The asteroid which recently burrowed its way into Jupiter was likely hundreds of times as large as whatever exploded over Tunguska. The Yucatan crash was a mere speck compared to Shoemaker-Levy, so how much warning would we realistically have? Even if we had warning, would it really do any good? How do you outrun an event with the potential to affect entire continents?

Luckily, even events in areas as remote as Tunguska get noticed. From the *lack* of similar reports through recorded

One of the few non-gratuitous chest exposure scenes to date.

human history, and by working in the statistics on population density, percentage of the planet covered by water, it's *statistically* unlikely that any asteroids will be slamming into a major city any time soon. And dedicated people are searching for anything threatening. Even as this article is written, NEAT, the Near-Earth Asteroid Tracking project, has identified seven "earth-crossers," including one nearly three kilometers across. How the threat would be handled if such a monster headed this way is a good question, perhaps even a justification for the thousands of hours, and significant funds, invested in the exploration of a few dead trees in Siberia. If nothing else, Tunguska, the mystery that's kept scientists guessing for almost a century, has been our warning.

CASE NOTES:
The Case for Life on Mars

It's perhaps ironic that this episode of *The X-Files* should combine the appearance of rocks reputedly proving that Mars once held life with the devastation of the Tunguska Event. Ironic in the sense that some scientists are already speculating that, if life did once arise on Mars, it may have been undone by a series of meteor and asteroid impacts that, except for magnitude, would have occurred much the way they did in Siberia.

Those "Martian canals," which inspired turn-of-the-century science fiction writers like H.G. Wells, have, for the past century, been put off as chance formations that should in no way suggest there are little green men tending a huge Martian garden, as the fiction suggested. However, from the beginning, scientists wondered if, sometime in Mars's distant past, those formations weren't indeed made by running water. And, where there's running water, so biologists tell us, there is at least the possibility, no matter how extreme, of life arising.

On the assumption that water did once cover a significant portion of the Martian surface, many scientists have forwarded

CASE CREDITS

WRITTEN BY: Chris Carter and
	Frank Spotnitz
DIRECTED BY: Kim Manners
ORIGINAL PRODUCTION
	NUMBER: 4X09
ORIGINAL US AIR DATE: 11/24/96

GUEST CAST

PRISONER
	Stefan Arngrim
FIRST COURIER
	David Bloom
CIGARETTE-SMOKING MAN
	William B. Davis
MARITA COVARRUBIAS
	Laurie Holden
CHAIRMAN
	Campbell Lane
ALEX KRYCEK
	Nicholas Lea
WELL-MANICURED MAN
	John Neville
TIMOTHY MAYHEW
	Brent Stait
DR. SACKS
	Malcolm Stewart
SENATOR SORENSON
	Fritz Weaver
AGENT PENDRELL
	Brendan

DEATH TOLL

1 MAN: stung to death

theories about where it went. Some link it to the "carbon cycle" here on Earth. Our atmosphere includes significant amounts of carbon dioxide, the carbon component of which comes from the exposed surfaces of rocks. They postulate that Mars may have lost part of its atmosphere to the carbon cycle, that the carbon, for whatever reason, remained locked in the rocks. Without an atmosphere, there's nothing to maintain the "greenhouse" that regulates temperature and keeps our water liquid and useable by carbon-based life forms.

Others theorize that solar winds gradually wore away Mars's atmosphere molecule by molecule until the buffer completely disintegrated, allowing water to follow the atmosphere, leaving only that water that was already frozen in Mars's visible polar caps. It's this sort of scenario that environmentalists frequently cite when warning the public of the effects of ozone depletion.

As the Martian canals appear to be some 3.5 to 4 million years old, some even speculate that a civilization much like our own could have arisen, poisoned their planet and been destroyed as a result. Archeology on Earth, they argue, doesn't necessarily transfer to situations on Mars, a planet that can hardly be considered to have been "investigated" on the basis of a few soil samples and unmanned expeditions.

However, scientists at the University of Arizona have developed a different model, the impact model. At the time of the Martian canals, the impact rate was considerably higher than at present, with larger bolides (the collective term for meteors, asteroids, and comets) the norm. As seen when Shoemaker-Levey slammed into Jupiter, the impact of large bodies creates plumes that rise high above the atmospheric surface – and are lost forever by the planet! While all such models are dependent on literally dozens of assumptions, some of the models do seem to fall within the limits of "extreme possibility."

CODE NAME:

"Terma"

Case: XF-4X10-12-01-96

X CATCH IT? Although the episode credits list a "Timothy Mayhew," Mulder refers to the militia leader as "Terry Edward Mayhew." While the Mayhew probably is a nod to the new duo who joined the writing stable this season, the discrepancy between the Timothy and Terry doesn't fit. Both the Mayhews are women!

EYEWITNESS STATEMENT

"It is my natural inclination to believe that they [Congressmen] are acting in the best interest of the truth – but I am not inclined to follow my own judgment in this case."

Special Agent Dana Scully

CASE SUMMARY

Mulder continues to track the source of a mysterious rock that's associated with an even more mysterious black cancer. Meanwhile, "official channels" back in the United States are turning up the heat on Agent Scully who, in between the demands on her time and freedom occasioned by an incredibly inconvenient committee hearing, is trying to follow up her own leads towards yet another connection to a smallpox scenario that's becoming all too familiar.

CASE HISTORY:
The Woman: Gillian Leigh Anderson

VITAL STATISTICS:
DOB: August 9, 1968
PLACE OF BIRTH: Chicago, Illinois:
St. Mary's Hospital, Cook County
HEIGHT: 5' 3"
HAIR: Blond, currently dyed auburn
EYES: Blue-green
PARENTS: Rosemary and Edward
SIBLINGS: 1 sister, Zoe, and 1 brother, Aaron, both younger
MARITAL STATUS: Separated from Clyde Klotz
CHILDREN: One, Piper, a daughter who was born during the early part of the second season's filming, on September 25, 1994. Creative filming allowed Anderson's real-life and fictional personas to remain firmly separate.
DISTINGUISHING MARKS: A tattoo on her right ankle.
PETS: 1 Neapolitan mastiff named Cleo.

EDUCATIONAL INFORMATION:
● Attended Fountain Elementary, Grand Rapids, Michigan.
● Graduated from City High, Grand Rapids, Michigan, 1986.
● Attended DePaul University's prestigious Goodman Theater School, graduating as a Bachelor of Fine Arts.

● Studied at the National Theater of Great Britain at Cornell University, Ithaca, New York.

PROFESSIONAL INFORMATION:

Anderson's acting ambitions began back in Grand Rapids, where she became involved in community theater. While at DePaul University, she earned a role in *The Turning* (1988) but moved east – not west – at graduation, choosing to pursue a career in theater instead of film. Three years later she'd appeared in *The Philanthropist* at the Long Wharf Theater in New Haven and won a Theater World Award for her performance in a production of Alan Ayckbourn's *Absent Friends*, an impressive achievement in a role for which she had only a few weeks to study. A dip into television with *Home Fires Burning*, a talking book version of *Exit to Eden* and an episode of *Class of 96* (Episode 8, "The Accused") later, she was willing to consider taking an episode role. The character of Dana Scully, a bright woman who'd sacrificed nothing of her femininity to a demanding career, had an irresistible appeal.

Chris Carter had already decided Anderson was made for the role, and despite some "questions" from the network – they suggested casting someone "taller, leggier, skinnier [and] with a lot more chest" – Gillian Anderson was cast as Scully.

At the Second Annual Screen Actors' Guild Awards, where actors honour the best among them, Gillian Anderson was awarded the hefty statue as the best actress in a dramatic television program. Considering that Anderson hadn't actually believed the show would run beyond its original half season of preliminary episodes, had no experience of the daily grind of television production and wasn't prepared for the mental strain of attempting to appear "fresh" for take after take after take, she's already displayed a level of professionalism others in the field could learn from.

X BLOOPER! The nurse tucked in her patients at 8:15. Mulder and Scully arrive at the Convalescent Home at 9:32. Yet, when asked when the patients were last checked, she replies, "Four hours ago, at bedcheck."

OTHER RESIDENCES:

As a young woman, Gillian Anderson travelled widely, following her father, also an actor, from Puerto Rico to London to Grand Rapids and Chicago. She has since lived in New York City and Los Angeles and currently makes her home in North Vancouver, British Columbia, Canada.

EARLY AMBITIONS:

Archeologist, marine biologist.

Filmography

X-Files: The Movie (1998) – Special Agent Dana Scully

Hellcab (1997)

The Mighty (1997) – Loretta

"The Simpsons" [Springfield Files] (1997) – Voice of Special Agent Dana Scully

"Reboot" (1996) – Voice of Data Nully

"Future Fantastic" (1996) – Host

"The X-Files" (1993–present) – Special Agent Dana Scully

"Class of 96" [The Accused] – Unknown

The Turning (1992) – April Cavanaugh

In addition to film and TV roles, she narrated the talking books *Exit to Eden* by Anne Rice and *The X-Files: Ground Zero* by Kevin J. Anderson. Her voice was also chosen for the character of E.V.E. in the Microsoft CD game "Hellbender" and is part of the vocal accompaniment to the "Extremis" single by Hal for Virgin Records.

The Character: Dana Katherine Scully

PERSONNEL DOSSIER: #121-627-161

NAME: Dana Katherine Scully

POSITION: Special Agent, Department of Justice, Federal Bureau of Investigation

CURRENTLY ASSIGNED: The X Files

FBI ID#: 2317-616
CONTACT#S: (Home) 202-555-6431 (Cellular) 202-555-3564

PERSONAL INFORMATION:
DOB: February 23, 1964 (Later changed to November 21, 1964, in the episodes "Nisei" and "731.")
HEIGHT: 5'3"
HAIR: Red
EYES: Blue/green
MARITAL STATUS: Single/Never Married
DEPENDENTS: No
PARENTS: Father, Captain (Ret.) William Scully (deceased) Mother, Margaret Scully
SIBLINGS:Two brothers (one older, one younger) are both unremarkable. William Scully, Jr., currently serves in the US armed forces. Older sister, Melissa, known to entertain certain "New Age" philosophies, died from a single gunshot wound to the head. The incident occurred at the residence of Agent Scully and has been linked to habitual criminal Louis Cardinal, now deceased.
IN CASE OF EMERGENCY: Notify Margaret Scully (mother)
RELIGIOUS AFFILIATION: Roman Catholic
(N.B.: A Living Will is on file.)

EDUCATIONAL INFORMATION:
Agent Scully came to the Bureau after taking an undergraduate degree in physics from the University of Maryland before completing a medical degree. Graduated FBI Training Academy, Quantico, in 1992. (N.B.: Maintained open relationship with Instructor/Special Agent Jack Willis during training.)

WORK HISTORY (CHRONOLOGICAL):
- Completed Medical Residency
- Assigned Quantico Training Facility, Instructor

THESE ARE THE EASY ONES! TAKE A SINGLE POINT FOR EACH CORRECT ANSWER.

1. What was Mulder's Russian cellmate's job before being jailed?

2. Where did Dr. Bonita Charne-Sayre die?

3. What was Dr. Charne-Sayre's speciality?

4. On what charge was Scully jailed?

5. What did Krycek "lose" in Tunguska?

THESE WILL MAKE YOU THINK, SO GIVE YOURSELF TWO POINTS FOR A CORRECT RESPONSE.

6. Who chaired the committee before which Scully testified?

7. Where did the stolen truck's owner find Mulder?

8. For what agency did Dr. Charne-Sayre work?

9. What happened to the diplomatic pouch?

10. What alias did Krycek use when he infiltrated the militia?

Answers

ONE POINTERS:

1. A geologist.

2. In a stable.

3. Variola viruses, smallpox.

4. Contempt of Congress.

5. An arm, his left.

TWO POINTERS:

6. Mr. Romine.

7. Under a leaf pile.

8. The World Health Organisation.

9. It was stolen by Vassily Peskow.

10. Arntzen.

YOUR SCORE _____

- Assigned X-Files, Field Agent (March 6, 1992)
- Reassigned Quantico Training Facility, Instructor
- Reassigned X-Files, Field Agent

SUPERVISORY NOTES (CHRONOLOGICAL):

1. It is the hope of this department that Agent Scully, coming from, and to all appearances more dedicated to, a more "traditional" scientific approach, will be able to properly assess the quantitative value of Agent Mulder's work, while observing that agent's general deportment and state of mind.

2. During a recent interview, our debriefing agent had cause to believe that assigning Agent Scully to *The X-Files* may not have been as well advised as originally thought. While the agent continues, in general, to adhere to the criminal investigative techniques outlined as optimal by this office, a tendency to "open-mindedness" has been observed.

3. Following a job-related abduction by Duane Barry (a known psychotic whom we suspect to have been working with an accomplice), Agent Scully received treatment for her injuries and was encouraged to discuss the incident with the bureau's in-house psychiatric staff. As such appointments are covered by doctor–patient confidentiality, no information regarding those sessions is available at this time. Reports of her field capability continue to support her decision to return to her previous duties, but constant reviews of her case files will be continued for the present time. (N.B.: Until such time as Agent Scully is able to compile a description of the events of her abduction, X-File #73317 must remain open.)

4. Following the events on the Two Grey Hills reserve, which may have resulted in the death of her partner, it is the recommendation of the Office of Professional Conduct that Special Agent Dana Scully be given a mandatory leave of absence until the full details of her misconduct can be calculated. This summary action is justified under the OPC Articles of Review, and Agent Scully will complete her suspension of duty without pay or benefits due to the nature of

her insubordination and the direct disobedience of her superior agents.

5. Agent Scully has been reinstated. While her complicity in her partner's activities is evident, her involvement in his disappearance, in his unauthorized investigations or in his insubordination cannot be assessed at this time. Her involvement in his death is, of course, moot.

6. Following the intervention of the Japanese Diplomatic Corps, Special Agent Scully and Special Agent Mulder have been officially denied permission to continue any investigation of the death of Steven Zinnzser.

7. At the request of Special Agent Patterson, investigation into a possible attempt by Agent Scully to obstruct justice and a federal agent, Special Agent Fox Mulder, in the performance of his duties has begun.

8. Investigation was dropped due to lack of evidence and special circumstances.

9. An appeal lodged by Special Agent Dana Scully, and seconded by Assistant Director Walter S. Skinner, to continue the investigation into the death of Melissa Scully has been received. It will be handled along with other paperwork of its type.

10. Following a refusal by her partner, Agent Fox Mulder, Agent Scully sought approval to divulge information to writer Jose Chung, and such request, having no bearing on secured information, has been granted. Liaison is to be through the Bureau's Public Relations Department and to be in accordance with the Freedom of Information Act provisions.

11. Agent Scully asked for, and received, a three-day medical leave, but has since returned to active duty.

12. While participating in a Congressional hearing, Special Agent Scully, acting in her professional capacity, refused to answer questions put to her. In addition to the Contempt of Congress charge, which resulted in her temporary incarceration, the Office of Professional Conduct will, of course, be reviewing the case

Guess Mulder has managed to make himself persona non grata with yet another government.

X Instead of "THE TRUTH IS OUT THERE," the signature line in the episode's opening credits read "E PUR SI MUOVE." It's a phrase that's sometimes attributed to Galileo, who supposedly uttered it while being questioned by the Inquisition. The parallel between Galileo, who was defending his theory that the earth moved and didn't, as most people of his time believed, stand still while the sun swung around it, and The Dynamic Duo called to answer to the Congressional Committee about the likelihood, actually the mere possibility, of life somewhere else in the universe, is another of the wonderfully subtle touches worked into The X-Files.

and making suggestions for any professional consequences at that time.

13. Upon further investigation, and with the recommendation of her immediate superior, it has been determined that no action will be taken in the matter of the Congressional hearings.

14. Following the death of Leonard Betts, Agent Scully has been cleared of any negligence or responsibility in the incident.

15. Agent Scully has submitted her official report on the death of her partner, Agent Fox Mulder, and is expected to file the remainder of the report, her assessment of the value of the X-Files, in person before the Office of Professional Conduct.

CASE NOTES
Guest Filmography: Nicholas Lea

DOB: June 22, 1962
PLACE OF BIRTH: New Westminster, British Columbia, Canada
PROFESSIONAL EDUCATION: Gastown Actors' Studio / Beverly Hills Playhouse / Charles Conrad Studios
"John Woo's Once a Thief – The Series" (1997) – Victor Mansfield
"John Woo's Once a Thief" (1996) – Victor Mansfield
"Highlander" [Money No Object] (1996) – Cory Raines
"Sliders" [Into the Mystic] (1996) – Ryan
"Sliders" [Luck of the Draw] (1996) – Ryan
Bad Company (1995) – Jake
The Raffle (1995) – David Lake
"E.N.G." [Cutting Edge] (1994) – Jeffrey Leggett
"The X-Files" (1993– present) – Agent/Comrade Alex Krycek
"Highlander" [The Fighter] (1993) – Rodney
"The Commish" (1991) – Ricky Caruso
Xtro II: The Second Encounter (1990) – Baines
American Boyfriends (1989) – Ron
Also episodes of Taking the Falls, Jake and the Kid, Lonesome Dove, Robin's Hoods, The Hat Squad, Madison, North of 60, The Marshall and E.N.G.

CODE NAME:

"El Mundo Gira"

Case: XF-4X11-01-12-97

CASE SUMMARY

Mulder and Scully arrive to investigate the death of Maria Dorantes, a young illegal immigrant, and quickly find themselves slogging through contradictory evidence, Latino folktales, and a quickly rising death toll – including entire truckloads of goats. While Scully finds her answers in the lab, Mulder can't resist putting more than one "alien" spin on events.

CASE HISTORY
The Making of a Modern Myth

It peers from the shadows with a multitude of faces. It tantalizes with a dozen different tracks. It nibbles from a hoard of domesticated snacks. And it's only a few years old!

Unlike its northeastern cousin, the Jersey Devil, which starred as *The X-Files*'s Indigenous North American Mythical Beast in the first season, or the second season's Classically Olde Worlde vampire, or even the Ancient and Environmentally Correct Monster lurking in the third season episode "Quagmire," El Chupacabra, star of "El Mundo Gira," is a sort of Nouveau Creature. While dozens of unexplained events have been attributed to it retroactively, the new kid on the block first came to prominence in Puerto Rico as recently as the 1970s and, even there, it failed to be taken seriously until it moved down out of the remote hill regions and into the more populous coastal communities where it proceeded to terrify yet more neighborhoods.

Of course, part of the problem with locating the elusive critter was the amazing variety of guises it seemed to assume at will. While the goats, cats, dogs and even cows reputed to be its victims couldn't give a description of their attacker, El Chupacabra isn't particularly shy of human company. Yet, for all the supposedly-trustworthy eyewitnesses who've observed it in a variety of lighting conditions, no two ever seem to come up with matching descriptions!

Mamie Touveriers spotted it just outside her tiny house,

EYEWITNESS STATEMENT

"There was a noise like thunder, but very close. And then this lightning, very bright, it blinded me. And I fell to the ground. And then I felt the hot rain fall on me, and when I finally could open my eyes and see, I saw the dead goat, and then I saw Maria. She called my name, once. She was lying in a puddle of yellow rain. Something had eaten at her face. Then I held her in my arms, and then she died."

Eladio Buente, as translated by Agent Conrad Lozano

squat over the unmoving remains of her cat. She described it quite succinctly as a "fox with wings, red-eyed, with nimble hands." Suggestions that she'd seen one of the local bats were met with scorn, hadn't she lived on the island all her life? Didn't she know what a bat looked like? And didn't the silly fool questioning her realize that bats didn't stand on their hind legs to stare back at the window – and grin?

Enrique Torres saw a completely different sort of creature when he encountered El Chupacabra lying on a branch above his head, its tail twitching up and down to avoid touching Enrique's head as he passed below. It wasn't the critter's odd appearance that drew Torres's attention. Unbelievable as it sounds, he hadn't actually noticed the yard-long, cat-like animal with its brindled fur, long teeth, and huge webbed paws. He didn't even notice the odd hissing he later reported hearing as the thing almost purred with each breath. No, it was the unbearable stench exuded by El Chupacabra that alerted Enrique Torres to the presence lurking above him. On first catching a whiff of the rancid odor, he'd thought some animal had carried its prey into a tree and forgotten it. When he looked up into El Chupacabra's "glowing eyes and gaping mouth," however, he realized the stench was part and parcel of the bizarre animal itself. He'd barely gathered his wits when the smelly beast "blinked twice, then disappeared into the upper branches and on into the forest."

Perhaps the more recent experience of Antonio Torres, no relation to Enrique, explains how such disparate descriptions could be reconciled. Like Enrique, Antonio reported the horrible smell. He likened it to "fish left in the sun too long." And like Mamie, he found the creature perched atop its latest meal, this time one of the goats that gave El Chupacabra its name – Goatsucker. As the amazed man watched, the animal appeared to "grow twice as big," an illusion really, as it "fluffed long fur, both a short matted layer and a longer, furry layer" up around itself. If that wasn't startling enough, the next

Trivia Buster

11

THESE ARE THE EASY ONES! TAKE A SINGLE POINT FOR EACH CORRECT ANSWER.

1. What domestic animals was Maria responsible for?

2. What color was the rain that fell on the migrant workers?

3. What alias did Eladio Buente choose for himself?

4. From whom did Eladio beg a ride back to Mexico?

5. What was the relationship between Eladio and Gabrielle?

THESE WILL MAKE YOU THINK, SO GIVE YOURSELF TWO POINTS FOR A CORRECT RESPONSE.

6. Where had the migrant workers set up their camp?

7. What film did Mulder feel was "deeply flawed"?

8. What did Jose Feliciano, Juan Valdez, Cesar Chavez and Placido Domingo all have in common in this episode?

9. Technically, what common condition did the truck driver die of?

10. Where does Gabrielle work nights?

Answers

KEEP TRACK OF YOUR TOTAL SCORE.
SEE WHERE YOU'D END UP IN THE
X-FILEAN WORLD OF HIERARCHIES,
SHADOW GOVERNMENTS,
AND CONSPIRACIES.

ONE POINTERS:

1. A small herd of goats.

2. Yellow.

3. Erik Estrada.

4. El Barbero.

5. They were cousins.

TWO POINTERS:

6. San Joaquin Valley, California.

7. *Purple Rain*.

8. They were all aliases for illegal immigrants.

9. Athlete's Foot.

10. La Ranchera Market.

YOUR SCORE _____

---

change, "like a chameleon, from dark brown, to palest blond," effectively changed the Chupacabra from a striped creature to one almost uniform in color. Antonio speculates that the protective colorations would make it practically invisible in dappled shadows or in the hay fields around the properties of grazing animals.

What his observations don't account for, of course, is the fact that though there are indeed many known animals capable of altering their coloration or pattern of coloration, none of those creatures have *fur*! Octopi, chameleons, several types of nudibranchs, and several species of fish regularly change color but it's achieved through alterations in skin pigmentation. If the Chupacabra is covered by not one, but two layers of smelly fur, it's hard to imagine how even the most observant witness could possibly notice its skin.

Of course, there are witnesses, like Michael Pallon, who claim El Chupacabra is as bald as Assistant Director Walter S. Skinner – or your typical X-Filean alien. Complete with bulging black eyes, enlarged heads, and tiny mouths, Pallon's descriptions would warm the hearts of any ufologist. He saw two such creatures, standing approximately four feet tall, while inspecting his cattle on a warm summer morning and, after overcoming his natural shock, was amazed with the speed with which they took off into the surrounding undergrowth. "I was on horseback and, granted they got a bit of a jump on me, but I couldn't have caught 'em if I'd been right on them. They didn't so much run as, well, sort of glide in long, low hops, sort of like desert lizards."

So, with so many witnesses reporting such apparently different creatures, how can they all possibly be lumped together as a single entity known as the Chupacabra? It seems the definitive mark of The Goatsucker isn't its appearance at all, but, rather, what it does. Regardless of size or demeanor, all Chupacabra do the same thing, suck their victims dry and leave the corpses, often horribly mutilated, out in plain sight.

The subjects of their attacks include practically any locally available, warm-blooded, and unprotected critters that happen to be handy. While goats, their throats pierced with paired punctures and drained of blood, seem to be the preferred menu item, El Chupacabra takes down an amazing variety of prey. In one bizarre instance, a Florida woman claims to have struck an opossum while driving. Hauling off to the side, she jumped from her car and hurried back along the verge to see if the animal was dead or merely injured. Before she could reach it, another creature, which fits one of the extraterrestrial-type descriptions of El Chupacabra, leapt from the low grass to the side, snatched up the still wriggling body and promptly sank its tiny teeth into the opossum's throat! El Chupacabra hissed once at Ellen Vaurnes, then sped back into the grass with its prize.

As the tale of El Chupacabra spread from Puerto Rico, through Mexico and into the United States, paranormal investigators began commenting on how the attacks attributed to El Chupacabra resembled the cattle mutilations they'd previously been linking to alien interference or even experimentation. Though it's difficult to picture some of the smaller versions of the Puerto Rican monster wrestling a full-grown cow to the ground, the "alien" connection, perhaps because of the bizarre mental images it arouses, garnered adherents almost immediately.

With its spread to the American media circuit, El Chupacabra became something of an overnight sensation and, as it migrated west, descriptions poured in. So did possible explanations. Everything from a vampire bat to feral cats to feral monkeys was considered at some point during the hunt for the mysterious creature. Other scientists, however, have a different explanation, one that revolves around people, not some cryptozoological hunt, and one that fits rather nicely into the story-telling theme John Shiban wove into his own take on The Goatsucker.

X CATCH IT? For those who've been amazed at Scully's ability to conduct a foot chase in nearly any style shoe, she can't be faulted for the bogtrotters she wore when Mulder *warned* her she'd be hiking over hill and dale.

X Wondering why Scully is singing show tunes from "West Side Story"? Believe it or not, refrains from the production waft across *The X-Files* set on a fairly regular basis as Mitch Pileggi and David Duchovny serenade one another between takes!

Into Every Life A Little Rain May Fall

Considering the fact that it was *Scully's* umbrella those frogs were using as a trampoline in "Die Hand Der Verletzt," it's hard to understand why a little thing like yellow rain had her rolling her eyes in "El Mundo Gira." Of all the things Mulder has theorized in four years of investigation, yellow rain is actually one of the better documented oddities he could have tossed out for Scully's contemplation. Thanks in no small part to Charles Fort, the original Fortean investigator and a real life amalgam of both halves of the Dynamic Duo, literally hundreds of colored rainfalls have been reported from all over the world.

Most of these unusual events have yet to be explained but one of the best known examples of a yellow rain is all too understandable and, had Mulder suggested it, instead of extraterrestrial influences, might even have gained some credibility in his

Can you really picture this sombre crew singing show tunes between shots?

Anthropologists and folklorists recognized the uniquely Latin American touches given to otherwise Western thought many years ago. Studies of the richly textured, highly symbolic, and strangely captivating version of Roman Catholicism practised in Latin America have kept ethno-anthropologists intrigued for decades. Voodoo, as practised in the Caribbean, is another example of a tradition capable of making connections between apparently divergent material to create a belief system perfectly suited to the needs of its practitioners. While mythologies like El Chupacabra don't quite rate up there with major religions, they do retain the essence of the regions in which they arise and many ethnographers view the El Chupacabra legend as a once-in-a-lifetime opportunity to actually track the birth and growth of a folktale. Of course, they don't view El Chupacabra as a real, living, blood-letting entity, but as partner's eyes. "Yellow rain" is the euphemism used to describe an insidious chemical-bacterial warfare component that is thought to have been used over troops in southeast Asia, Afghanistan, Poland and dozens of other countries. While the exact composition of Yellow Rain remains something of a mystery itself, users of biological and chemical weapons not being noted for following a particular recipe if something more deadly should suggest itself, educated guessers are suggesting a primary chemical poison, a biological agent with a known limiting factor, and a secondary chemical which provides the biological agent with a little "boost" to ensure it contaminates ground water, food crops, even people. As the American government's record for testing unsuspecting subjects is well established in the wake of a rash of "official apologies" issued for everything from involuntary radiation experiments to the mish-mash made of a testing situation that actually exposed unsuspecting black men to lethal agents, Scully might well have accepted the possibility of a conspiracy this time around!

an amalgam of the fears, hopes and concerns of an area and its people drawn from both traditional and modern-day events.

Ethnographers point out that blood-sucking monsters seem considerably less incredible in a densely populated area that is home to all three species of the world's only true vampire bats! Though El Chupacabra is today's incarnation, other blood-suckers occur frequently in Hispanic literature and folktale and their exclusion might well be regarded as *more* unusual than the inclusion of such abilities. In the region just south of the Panama Canal, legends of a man-sized bat that walked upright and fed on the blood of small children who wandered away from their families were recorded in 1794! According to Daniel Sweeney, a folklorist involved in a nine-year project to document the traditional teaching stories of the area, "Every culture clothes its taboos in Bogeymen. Victorians told their

WRITTEN BY: John Shiban
DIRECTED BY: Tucker Gates
ORIGINAL PRODUCTION
NUMBER: 4X11
ORIGINAL US AIR DATE: 01/12/97

GUEST CAST

ASSISTANT DIRECTOR WALTER
S. SKINNER
  Mitch Pileggi
ELADIO BUENTE
  Raymond Cruz
SOLEDAD BUENTE
  Jose Yenque
GABRIELLE BUENTE
  Simi
CONRAD LOZANO
  Ruben Blades
MARIA DORANTES
  Pamela Diaz
FLAKITA
  Lillian Hurst
OLD SHANTY WOMAN
  Tina Amayo
RICK CULVER
  Mike Kopsa
DR. LARRY STEEN
  Robert Thurston
COUNTY CORONER
  Susan Bain

DEATH TOLL

4 MEN: 1 shot, 3 "death by mould"
1 WOMAN: "death by mould"

kids that masturbation made hair grow on your palms, which, at the time, was also an indication of were-ism, which included werewolves, werepigs, were-everythings. Blood-sucking is, for all practical purposes, a sub-form of cannibalism, one of the last remaining taboos. It'd be strange not to have some sort of folklore associated with it. In the early 1920s, there was a similar tale circulating, but, in that story, the blood-sucker was a female entity."

A high degree of symbolism surrounds most folktales, the El Chupacabra included. Ethnographers with a socio-economic slant to their work, however, take the term "blood-sucker" slightly less literally, pointing out that most of the vampiric-style tales evolve in countries where the native population perceives itself as victims. "When a larger nation, like the United States, abuts, and utilizes the resources of, a less privileged region, it's almost inevitable that a blood-sucking folktale will arise fairly quickly," says Peter Montreso, a Mexico City anthropologist. "The facts are these, the Americans pay much less for labor in their factories here than back home, they pay less for equivalent resources, and they tend to be incredibly protectionist about civil rights within their boundaries, inversely unconcerned with what happens in the countries they see as 'satellite resource states.' If you track the progress of El Chupacabra stories within the United States itself, you'll see that it's a socio-economic trail that leads the Goatsucker from region to region. The lower stratum of American society feels the same pressures that a laborer in Columbia feels, has the same monetary stress as working Hondurans, and about as much security as a Guatemalan family. These people literally feel as if their lifeblood, their hope, their resources are being torn away from them. The Chupacabra reflects that."

And how do witnesses of the Chupacabra react to such highbrow commentaries? "Well," shrugs Sophe-Maria Torres, "I suppose they need some way to rationalize it to themselves."

CODE NAME:

"Kaddish"

Case:XF-4X12-02/16/97

EYEWITNESS STATEMENT

"The early cabalists believed that a righteous man could actually create a living being from the earth itself, fashioned from mud or clay – but this creature could only be brought to life by the Power of the word"

Judaic Archivist

CASE SUMMARY

An apparent series of hate crimes brings Mulder and Scully to one of New York City's ethnic communities where an Hasidic Jew, violently murdered, is being implicated in the deaths of his attackers! The contradiction has Scully groping for explanations that nearly defy even Mulder's range of "extreme possibilities" – until a Judaic text bursts into flame and Mulder begins gathering evidence that a creature out of folklore has come to life.

CASE HISTORY
Ashes to Ashes, Dust to Dust . . . Mud to Mud?

Creation stories connect all people, all cultures, all histories. At some point, various groups of human beings looked at one another, at the world around them, and wondered, "How did we come to be?" In .many ways, it was our asking questions, curious thoughts put into words, that defined us as human. Nearly all creation stories share something in common – the belief that humanity comes from the mud of this world and that it is imbued with life only by some divine spark.

The story of the golem is a morality play, a creation story, history, philosophy, alchemy and theology all rolled into one. In the earliest instances of the story, when Abraham and his teacher, Shem the son of Noah, studied the *Sefer Yetzirah*, they discovered a series of hidden meanings within the phrases and numbers and, in deciphering these hidden truths, realized that their meditations and contemplations of the meanings brought them close to an understanding of the Divine, to understanding creation itself. Though their study led them to animate a calf, not a man, the calf was whole and complete and the reader is given to understand that, at that moment of creation, they could as easily have brought planets and universes into being. Heavy stuff.

When Abba Ben Rav Hamma, better known as Rava, took

up his studies of the mystical book, he began his meditations with the Rabbi Zera and, between them, the two men appear to have achieved a level of understanding equal to Abraham and Shem's because, after many years, they too animated a calf. Nor were they alone. Study and meditation guided many historic figures towards the Book of Creation as they sought a closer communion with their creator. Rabbis Hanina and Hoshia took their study of the *Sefer Yetzirah* seriously and regularly, resulting in a habitual diet of young calf for their Sabbath suppers.

But human beings, being human, couldn't see calves as the pinnacle of achievement. If, as the Talmud and Koran suggested, any golem created by a person would remain incomplete, incapable of speech, without the input of a deity, how would an animated calf really differ from an ordinary calf? It seems the same question presented itself to Rava as well and, before long, his contemplations turned from livestock to the creation of a human golem.

Unfortunately, according to the Talmud, Rava's curiosity and study now took a turn from the approved curriculum as laid out in the *Sefer Yetzirah* and other mystical texts. Like all creation tales, this one comes complete with not only expectations of power, but the possibility of ruin. Golems weren't just elaborate mud pies. Though without soul, they were expected to take on the characteristics and purpose of their maker. (The early discussions of golems never referred to the deceased because, in most cases, the golem was a creation of the maker's imagination, not an animation of a specific individual.) Caution after caution warned students of the absolute necessity for a "purity of purpose" and of the dozens of small errors, in spirit as well as physical form, that could result in the creation of a monster – foremost among the list of "Do Nots" was a prohibition against *individuals* attempting to breath life into the clay creatures. While a group engaged in active study

Trivia Buster

12

THESE ARE THE EASY ONES! TAKE A SINGLE POINT FOR EACH CORRECT ANSWER.

1. What sort of business did Isaac Luria run?

2. What happened to the book Mulder found in Luria's casket?

3. What flag was hanging in the back room of Curt Brunjes's print shop?

4. Whose fingerprints were found on Tony Oliver's throat?

5. Where was Isaac Luria buried?

THESE WILL MAKE YOU THINK, SO GIVE YOURSELF TWO POINTS FOR A CORRECT RESPONSE.

6. What was the title of the pamphlet shoved under the Weisses' door?

7. What was stamped on the Sefer Yetzirah found in the casket?

8. What did Jacob Weiss bring to New York from Europe?

9. What did Mulder find on Jacob's cuff?

10. What was Ariel Weiss wearing in the synagogue?

12

could provide some focus, some protection, for its members, a single person might easily find himself a victim of his own, hidden and unacknowledged, desires.

When Rava, working alone, created his human golem, he sent it immediately to the home of his former colleague, Rabbi Zera, who, apparently, accepted it as a genuine man – until he tried to speak with it. The "words as things of power" theme winding its way through the episode "Kaddish" is as intrinsic a part of the golem tale as its origin in common clay. It was the Talmudic golem's lack of language that alerted Rabbi Zera to the fact that this "man" wasn't a man at all and it was with language, "Return to dust," that Zera dismissed Rava's creation. That Rava would study the *Sefer Yetzirah* alone, particularly the sections on golem creation, remains as something of an oddity in Judaic tradition, and perhaps explains the easy way Zera deconstructed it. That Rava would send it to Zera in the first place, however, makes perfect sense and shouldn't be considered an act of ill will on Rava's part – or not intentional ill will. Such creations were, historically, nothing more than an indication that the student had mastered the *Sefer Yetzirah*, sort of the ultimate comprehensive examination. Perhaps it was a renunciation of Rava's lone study that results in there being no record of just how he accomplished the creation of his golem.

With the exception of Rava's creation, however, the processes for animating a golem, and there are several, have been laid out in a number of sources in such seemingly straightforward language that many scholars follow the theory that there never were any physical golems! Instead, they postulate that the moment of understanding creation, when a man would perceive the means to create the golem, had the same weight, theologically, as actually animating a clay figure. It was enough to simply know.

The people of Prague probably wouldn't have agreed with that, however. In the 1500s, the life of a Jew in Prague made

The powerful images of this episode are second only to the unforgettable music Mark Snow created for it.

X A bit more of the name game in action in "Kaddish." The character Isaac Luria was named for a 16th-century Kabbalist whose students wrote extensively on the numerological and astrological basis for the work found in the Book of Creation and other Judaic texts.

living in 1990s Brooklyn look like a cakewalk. While Brooklyn's community undoubtedly faces accusations of usury and worse, few people would publicly suggest the residents of Williamsburg were killing Christian babies on a regular basis to make up some *matzot* for Passover – a charge that resulted in hundreds of Jews from Prague being accused of murder! The situation became so dire that, in 1572, Rabbi Judah Loew, along with his son, Rabbi Isaac ha-Kohen, and his student, Rabbi Ya'aqov Sason ha-Levi, contrived to create a physical golem of their own to protect the Jewish ghetto. Like the golem created in "Kaddish," this one sprang from an interpretation of the 72 letter-names of God. It went out into the community and, where Jews had once been attacked, the gentiles of Prague began to die. How long this went on varies from account to account, but, in most versions, it had become pretty bloody before the Jews approached Rabbi Loew and suggested that some other solution might be well-advised.

Once again in company with his son and students, Rabbi Loew went before the council of Prague and put forth a number of resolutions including laws that upheld a Jew's right to defend himself against charges laid against him (a right he

X CATCH IT? Though Scully correctly identifies the Irgun as a clandestine Israeli military group, it's highly unlikely the British, or anyone else, were arresting its members in the 1950s. Israel became a state before that and the Irgun's membership was promptly taken into the mainstream Israeli army and considered war heroes by many in 1959.

X Wonder where that hate literature originated? The Anti-Defamation League can also attest to the fact that such literature is often boilerplate, the same text with a different group's or nationality's particulars filled into the blanks. Precisely the same pamphlets have appeared with phrasing for Asians (the Yellow Plague), blacks, and homosexuals.

didn't have at the time), that his Rabbi be present during his accusation and defence (a sensible notion as the Judaic faith made little distinction between the law-giving and priestly functions), and that the accusor be made to prove his case (until then the accused was assumed to be guilty). While life in Prague remained difficult for 16th-century Jews, it improved vastly when it became illegal for them to be killed in the street.

NOTEBOOK

Blasts from the Past

Considering the care given to recreating the feeling and details of a Judaic community, it's hard to understand how *The X-Files's* fact-checkers could have come to the conclusion that either Yankel Rosenbaum or Tawana Brawley was connected to Williamsburg . . .

Yankel Rosenbaum, stabbed to death in apparently mindless retaliation for the death of Gavin Cato, a black child who was hit by a car driven by an Hasidic Jew (a man completely unknown to Rosenbaum), was a *visitor* to the United States. Originally from Melbourne, Australia, he was residing in Crown Heights at the time of his death. While Crown Heights is in Brooklyn, there's a ton of space between Williamsburg and Crown Heights.

Of course, Tawana Brawley wasn't even in New York City, much less Williamsburg. The black woman who claimed to have been assaulted, *raped*, and covered with slurs written in excrement, was a resident of Wappingers Falls, some sixty or so miles away. Her case, brought against six white men, was found to be without foundation.

Though residents of the Williamsburg area haven't been immune to incidents of racial hatred and tensions, neither Tawana Brawley nor Yankel Rosenbaum was involved.

The story of Prague's golem isn't just an example of the historic oppression of the Jews, it's also instructive in its details and reveals a great deal about how golems and their creation were perceived. While the golem in "Kaddish" seems to have been created almost on a whim, by a single person, the golem in Prague required considerable preparation. Taking the astrological and alchemical aspects of Judaic mysticism into account, Rabbi Loew chose his assistants on the basis of their birth signs. He was born under an Air constellation, his son-in-law was born under a Fire sign, and he chose a student who was of the Water constellations to complete the trio. The golem itself, made from a suitable type of clay, was, understandably, considered capable of standing for the Earth elements. Even with this mystic requirement satisfied, the three men didn't rush straight out to prepare their clay man. Instead, they spent a week in contemplation, fasting, and prayer to purify their minds, bodies and souls. They firmly believed that the golem, lacking any of its own aspirations, would take on those of its creators. If the "Kaddish" golem is assumed to have followed the model in the Prague legend, it would seem that, on some level, Ariel Weiss wanted retribution for the loss of her husband, even if her golem seemed independent enough to try hanging her father, something it's unlikely she would have desired.

Another part of the Prague golem's story involves Rabbi Loew's wife and her perceptions of the creature her husband brought home and introduced as a mute. The obvious inference is that, unlike other media interpretations of a golem, *The X-Files* may have been right on the money in depicting their golem as not only humanoid but recognizable as a specific person. In the Prague legend, no one questioned the nature of the golem once it was properly clothed and the markings on its forehead (an equally traditional location for the letters) covered.

X Many X-Philes were struck by the one note of color in the opening frames, the young girl in the red coat, and couldn't help but be reminded of the film *Schindler's List*. When Jacob Weiss is revealed as having been a child with nimble fingers capable of working on munitions, the plot link to *Schindler's List* caught even those viewers who missed the teaser.

X X-Philes who'd seen Gillian Anderson's appearance on the Jay Leno show, which featured a blooper excerpt of the many times the Book of Creation *failed* to burst into flames – despite Duchovny's valiant efforts, which included a burst of heavy breathing – couldn't help chuckling when the on-air version went up right on cue!

CASE CREDITS

WRITTEN BY: Howard Gordon
DIRECTED BY: Kim Manners
ORIGINAL PRODUCTION
    NUMBER: 4X12
ORIGINAL US AIR DATE: 02/16/97

GUEST CAST
RABBI
    David Freedman
HASIDIC MAN
    Murrey Rabinovitch
ARIEL LURIA
    Justine Miceli
ISAAC LURIA
    Harrison Coe
JACOB WEISS
    David Groh
DEREK BANKS
    Channon Roe
TONY
    Timur Karabilgin
CLINTON BASCOMBE
    Jabin Litwiniec
CURT BRUNJES
    Jonathan Whittaker
KENNETH UNGAR
    David Wohl
DETECTIVE
    George Gordon

DEATH TOLL
5 MEN: 1 shot, 3 strangled and
    1 hung

The purity of purpose comes up again when Rabbi Loew asks that his wife not give the new member of their family any menial tasks – not even to draw water from the well for her. Another version of the golem story emphasized this particular no-no by having the golem nearly drown the mistress who'd set him to work. *The Sorcerer's Apprentice*, a Disney film featuring Mickey Mouse as a novice mage who animates a broomstick to carry water for him, is a modern interpretation of the golem tale that still revolves around the fact that golems aren't intended for everyday tasks. In the story of Prague's golem, Rabbi Loew is horrified to discover that his wife has set his golem to work for her and quickly removes the creature from her house. If *The X-Files*'s golem acts a little contrary to more traditional versions, perhaps it's because of its unusual creation. Whatever other purposes Ariel might have had, it's obvious that her overwhelming motive was to hang on to someone she loved, the most prosaic, romantic, commonplace, and inappropriate reason possible.

The "death" of *The X-Files*'s golem, however, might have come straight from the Prague tale. Both golems returned to dust high inside a synagogue, at the hands of their creator. The Prague golem is rumoured to lie in the same loft even now, though no one is supposed to have opened the sealed door to the room in several centuries. For those who tend to favor the more mystical, less physical version of a golem, it's interesting to note that, amid the hundreds of toppled headstones in Prague's Judaic cemeteries, Rabbi Judah Loew's is one of only a handful still standing. The synagogue said to house the golem's remains still stands in Prague's ghetto – despite the utter destruction of almost every Jewish shrine and meeting hall under Hitler's even harsher oppression.

Jews hid there in the darkest days of World War II and survived.

CODE NAME:

"Never Again"

Case: XF-4X13-02-02-97

EYEWITNESS STATEMENT

"I hear her, Dana. In my head, only deeper. It's more than just some chemical reaction. She talks to me."

Edward Jerse

CASE SUMMARY

Mulder is on forced vacation, leaving Scully to follow up on a case she already believes to be completely spurious. As she trails his suspect/source, she has plenty of time to contemplate her career choices, her relationship with her father, her relationship – or lack thereof! – with Mulder, and her complete lack of a social life. As a growing sense of dissatisfaction nudges her towards an impulsive weekend's amusement, circumstances conspire to draw her back to the world of forensics, violence and investigations of the bizarre – only this time she's not the investigator, she's one of the subjects!

CASE HISTORY

The History of Ergot: From Witch's Brew to High-Tech High to Respectable Pharmaceutical

The X-Filean writing team's deft touch for both the poetic and the ironic was working overtime when Scully, in attempting to leave her workday world behind, instead found herself personally entangled in an X File firmly rooted in her precious science, and victim to the same compound which may well have started the Salem Witch Trials. The history of humanity's relationship with ergot, a mushroom with a taste for cereal grains, is actually, in one sense, something of an allegory of both Mulder and Scully's quest to bring his paranormal passions into mainstream investigations. Medicine has been alternating between praising and cursing the effects of ergot almost since humanity first cultivated grains – and its fantastic appearances are still keeping scientists hopping.

If Scully had been a midwife in ancient Greece instead of a modern-day North American doctor, she, and the rest of her female colleagues, would likely have been several centuries ahead of the acknowledged physicians of the time. While the men argued politics as part of their medical practise, the women were busy cataloguing an impressive collection of folk remedies. When Hippocrates was still working out just how blood travelled from one part of the body to the others, famous seers and prophetesses were inducing their visions and a class of women students were learning how the lowly ergot could prevent deaths caused by post-partum haemorrhaging. Those same women also knew that, in careful doses, ergot could end an unwanted pregnancy without killing the mother and, in even more restricted amounts, could induce labor if a baby was significantly overdue. Formal medical practitioners wouldn't discover ergot's healthful applications for over a thousand years until midwives in China reintroduced the knowledge that had been lost in Greece. Europeans didn't learn of it until sometime early in the 1500s when the bizarre little drug was taken onto French battlefields in an attempt to keep men from bleeding to death before they could receive serious medical attention – and still most physicians failed to realize it was the same drug they'd been fighting against for centuries! Some remnant of herbal folklore seemed to have survived in Germany, however, where tales of a demon "corn mother" stalking the fields and loosing her "corn wolves," ergotism, on the populace survive to the present day. In fact, two German names for ergot, *seigle ivre*, "drunken rye," and *tollkorn*, "mad grain," suggest that, though scientists and physicians remained puzzled, the common people had already made some connections, even if only through folklore, between the fungus, the illness and madness.

The medicinal applications and the illnesses, however, were seldom combined and, until that happened in the 1800s, ergot was best known for the numerous maladies, some approaching the destructive ability of plagues, that it brought to the European continent. Though it would take modern-day physicians and agronomists to fully understand how the same little fungus that could easily decimate entire populations could also save hundreds of lives, the effects of *Claviceps purpurea* were easily diagnosed. In fact, *three* separate categories of ergotism have been recognized since 1420.

Trivia Buster

13

THESE ARE THE EASY ONES! TAKE A SINGLE POINT FOR EACH CORRECT ANSWER.

1. What was written on Ed Jerse's tattoo?

2. What did Scully take away from the Vietnam Veterans' Memorial?

3. How long had it been since Mulder took a vacation?

4. Which color did Scully admire in Ed's tattoo?

5. To what cartoon does Scully compare Mulder's latest case?

THESE WILL MAKE YOU THINK, SO GIVE YOURSELF TWO POINTS FOR A CORRECT RESPONSE.

6. What game does Mulder suggest they play if Scully gets a desk?

7. What was the first word Betty said to Ed Jerse?

8. Where does Mulder's "spiritual journey" take him?

9. For what firm did Ed work before getting fired?

10. How did Betty describe Scully?

Trivia Buster

13

That an eruption of gangrenous ergotism could result in a whole family being burned alive inside their home becomes less shocking, less reprehensible, when the ravages the disease inflicted are appreciated. Victims of this version of ergot poisoning stumbled about on limbs that were literally dying, their supply of oxygenated blood cut off by ever constricting blood vessels. Just as true gangrene attacks living tissue, poisoning it, gangrenous ergotism turns healthy bodies into putrid masses. Formerly hale arms and legs quickly lost circulation, blackened, shrivelled and took on an almost mummified appearance. It wasn't unusual for these abused appendages to snap off at the joints. No one knew what caused it and, most tragically, no one realized it *wasn't* contagious. At a time when epidemics and plagues were destroying towns as often as individuals, few communities could be persuaded to care for ergotism victims. Most, in blind panic at the horrific spectacle presented by shambling, deformed ergot victims, reacted violently and found no reason to regret their decisions.

One town in southern France recorded an outbreak of gangrenous ergotism in the fall of 1543 with a notation to the effect that, "Four homes beyond the pale of the Abbey of St. Bartholomew were put to the torch today when the monks, the only souls to offer the victims solace, withdrew from the tiny embankment upon which the sufferers were confined." Rather than let the sick come into contact with anyone, the town leaders ordered the monks to stay inside the abbey until the disease disappeared then, under cover of darkness, forced those still alive into a storage shed which burned to the ground in less than an hour.

The other well-recorded type, convulsive ergotism, received little more tolerance. The seizures which give this form of the disease its name were violent and frightening. Frothing of the mouth, tongue biting (even biting completely through the tongue), fierce bouts of nausea, ravenous hunger, unrelenting thirst and bouts of choking, gasping apnoea were common symptoms and swiftly reduced victims to wasted versions of their former selves. Nerve damage, another common side effect, left those who survived with spasmodic movements, sensory impairment and permanent deformities. And many didn't survive at all. Small wonder, really, that few people were willing to care for these pathetic patients. It's estimated that, between 995 and 1000, some 250,000 people died of some form of ergotism.

One group that did just that, however, also indirectly provided convulsive ergotism's other, more colorful names, names like "Holy Fire," *ignis sacer*, and St. Anthony's Fire. Just as other orders of monks, particularly the Benedictines, had supported hospices dedicated to victims of leprosy and organic-cause insanity, another order, who took St. Anthony as their patron, provided one of the rare respites for ergotism victims inside shrines whose front doors were painted brilliant red. The "fire" refers not only to the painful effects of ergotism on the victims' flesh, but their unquenchable thirst. In his 1602 diary, a priest of the Order of St. Anthony, Brendan Breimer, records the decision of one unusually sympathetic judge who, to punish a young boy for his harassment of his afflicted neighbor, forced him to fetch as much water as his neighbor might ask for, whenever he might ask for it, regardless of weather or season. Considering the fact that their communal well was a mile and a half distant from either farm, it was no easy penance and certainly would have driven home the desperate situation of ergotism victims.

The third form of ergotism, one that frequently accompanied one of the first two, and that may – or may not – have afflicted the recently divorced Ed Jerse in "Never Again," is hallucinogenic ergotism. Like Jerse, victims heard voices, saw visions, and described being seized by strange compulsions which they could only watch themselves acting out, apparently

X Gillian Anderson does indeed have a real-life tattoo, though not one of a snake eating itself. About an inch wide and two inches long, the Tahitian tribal design that decorates the inside of her right ankle is usually hidden by flesh-colored tape during filming.

X CATCH IT? That wasn't just any old "Entertainment Weekly" cover that ended up in the bird cage. The mock up, a jab at the magazine that dared laugh at "The Field Where I Died," featured a cover photo of Co-Executive Producer Robert Goodwin above "The Wisest Man In Hollywood?"

X BLOOPER! Scully's last date couldn't have been in 1992. The episode "The Jersey Devil," which takes place in 1993, showed us Scully's last known dinner date – and illustrated at least two table conversations to avoid on a successful date: autopsies and your last divorce.

X This episode, originally slotted to appear in the coveted time period immediately following the American Superbowl, was also originally scheduled to have a different director. Quentin Tarantino, Hollywood's Bad Boy Director, usually works in film but was given an exemption from the Directors Guild of America to direct an episode of "ER" last season. The Guild had assumed Tarantino would eventually get his Guild status in order. When he didn't, they quickly nixed any notions of a second exemption to film *The X-Files* episode "Never Again."

powerless to regain control of their thoughts. And it was insidious. If hallucinogenic ergotism appeared without any of the symptoms common to its convulsive and gangrenous cousins, few people, including the victim, would even realize they were ill!

Just such an situation may well have been responsible for the "witch-mania" that gripped Salem and other communities

NOTEBOOK

A Snake By Any Other Name

Those fans generous enough to see the historical symbolism inherent in the tattoo Scully adopts in this episode – and not just another blatant attempt to push FOX's latest Chris Carter production, *Millennium* – will quickly be rewarded by discovering the snake's common roots in half a dozen geographically and ethnically separated traditions.

The Oroboros, in some Native American myths, represents not only time but the apparently opposing traits of constancy and change. Constancy for the stability the Earth enjoys for as long as Oroboros continues to grip its tail and keep chaos at bay. Change for the inevitable march of time that brings seasons and growth.

In the Judeo-Christian mythos, the Leviathan once coiled itself around the world, gripping its tail in its teeth to await the Day of Judgement when it will battle Behemoth, its ancient enemy. According to prophesy, neither of the great reptiles will survive, but, while Behemoth is cast into darkness, Leviathan provides sustenance for the rebirth of humanity so it, in some sense, lives on.

The earliest Greek myths also include the story of the snake Umbrae. It also wrapped itself around the world just before swallowing its tail and turning into a ring of mountains protecting the new-born world.

in the 1690s. As recorded in a number of diaries of the time, the rye harvest had been late, with the grains collected while it was either hot and sultry or cold and damp, in other words, perfect conditions for the widespread growth of ergot. The convulsive visions suffered by the three children who identified the first "witches," the voices others claimed to have heard during the night, and the bizarre behavior of some of those accused can easily be seen, in hindsight, to have been symptomatic of hallucinogenic ergotism. The sudden end to the visions and accusations also coincides rather nicely with the end of that year's rye crop. Though less well-known, a similar instance of unexplainable mania towards so-called witches broke out in Kryznia in 1723. Thirteen women and one young girl died before the community "came to its senses." A monument to the dead is encircled by stone sheaves of rye.

While cases of "St. Anthony's Fire" do still erupt from time to time, usually in association with a war or famine that forces people to eat grains they'd have rejected in more prosperous times, ergot has now moved from the realm of folklore into labs both amateur and professional. Ergot's mind-altering properties, which the Germans noted fairly early, were "discovered" by Dr. Albert Hofmann in 1938 when he derived lysergic acid diethylamide-25, LSD, from ergot. His original chemical would be reproduced, altered and cut by hundreds of less-skilled biochemists and become one of the most potent psychogenic drugs ever to hit the black market. In a move that would have shocked ergot victims of just a few centuries ago, modern generations ingested one of ergot's multitude of derivatives for *pleasure*! The disjoint, powerless feeling dreaded by those treated by the Order of Saint Anthony was welcomed by a generation perfectly willing to view themselves from the outside.

Not surprisingly, it would take a few more years to get ergot back into labs looking for its medicinal value, but, following

Any number of X-Philes would like to get this close to Gillian Anderson.

X The Vietnam Memorial where Scully finds her rose petal is actually a mock-up of the original. This scene, like the rest, was actually filmed in Vancouver.

CASE CREDITS

WRITTEN BY: Glen Morgan and
   James Wong
DIRECTED BY: Rob Bowman
ORIGINAL PRODUCTION
   NUMBER: 4X13
ORIGINAL US AIRDATE: 02/02/97

GUEST CAST

ED JERSE
   Rodney Rowland
ED'S LAWYER
   Peter Nadler
ED'S EX
   Jen Forgie
ED'S DIVORCE JUDGE
   Carla Stewart
DETECTIVE GOUVEIA
   Jay Donahue
DETECTIVE SMITH
   Ian Robison
VSEVLOD PUDOVKIN
   Igor Morozov
MS. HADDEN
   Jan Bailey Mattia
MS. VANSEN
   Rita Bozi
MRS. SHIMA-TSUNO
   Marilyn Chin
BARTENDER
   Barry "Bear" Horton
KAYE SCHILLING
   Jillian Fargey
HANNAH
   B.J. Harrison
RUSSIAN STORE OWNER
   Natasha Vasiluk
COMRADE SVO
   Bill Croft

DEATH TOLL

1 WOMAN: method unknown

the initial success of several physicians exploring its traditional use as an anti-haemorrhagic, a variety of modern pharmaceuticals have arisen. Ergotamine takes advantage of ergot's effect on blood flow, making it a remarkable effective treatment for migraine headaches. Hydergine, likewise noted for improving blood flow, is regularly administered to stroke and epilepsy sufferers and, in Italian studies, has shown some effectiveness in restoring the alertness and memory of elderly patients. Ergonovine, a refined version of ergot without its nastier side-effects, is still used to prevent bleeding in women who've just given birth. Ergosterol, a more recent application, is believe to be converted to a particularly useful form of Vitamin D.

From food of the Greek mystics, to abortifacient, to unwitting cause of the witch trials, to the "holy fire" of a medieval plague, to underground psychedelic, to modern pain reliever, the lowly ergot traces an incredible history through science and those precursors to the paranormal, folklore and witchcraft.

CODE NAME:

"Leonard Betts"

Case: XF-4X14-01-26-97

CASE SUMMARY

When the decapitated body of an EMT just disappears from the morgue of a local hospital, Mulder is all set to track down his own version of the Headless Horseman. Scully isn't buying any of it and, on discovering the missing head in an industrial-sized waste management unit, promptly suggests a far more likely candidate – body snatchers. Unfortunately for Scully, however, a disturbing trail of physical evidence, evidence she herself helped establish, is doing nothing to further her theory!

CASE HISTORY
The Extremes of Possibility . . . And Beyond!

The X-Files has pushed the extremes of possibility before, and will undoubtedly have us all scratching our heads again before long, but, "Leonard Betts" was one of the few episodes to leave us rolling in the aisles! The Headless EMT rides again! And Mulder... Well, the FBI is clearly putting out a unique range of agents who can walk into a morgue, eyeball some footprints on the inside of a refrigeration unit, and immediately infer that they're chasing a Monster of the Week with a taste for cancerous bits of laboratory waste. But, like *kitsch*, things that are so ugly they're actually cute, "Leonard Betts" was so far beyond the extremes of possibility that, once we stopped laughing, we could ignore the science and just settle in for a scary-gory-stand-alone episode with more caustic one-liners flying in a single show than had tickled our funny bone for the previous half-dozen episodes. It was camp, it was drama, it was *The X-Files*!

A *Calgary-Herald* writer once commented that "*The X-Files* takes tabloid news, crosses it with the best of Billy Crystal, then runs it through the same dramatic engine that powers *ER* and *NYPD Blue* – there's nothing more dramatic, but it always starts in the tabloids!" The number of Elvis jokes and mocked up supermarket-counter headlines that have appeared in *The X-Files*'s first four seasons certainly acknowledges the camp

EYEWITNESS STATEMENT

"What if there was a case where the cancer was not caused by damaged DNA, where the cancer was – was not a destructive or an aggressive factor, but was rather the normal state of being? . . . What if this man's life force, his *chi*, whatever you want to call it, somehow retained blueprint' of the actual man himself, guiding rampant growth, not as cancer, but as regeneration!"

Special Agent Fox Mulder

element that helps keep the otherwise darkling tale from sending viewers off to slit their wrists each week. But, with that heritage in mind, articles like these – taken to the next degree – could all be X files!

From Melbourne, Australia: A forty-seven-year-old man racing naked down the street is promptly arrested for public indecency. The judge, however, declared the man was entirely justified in his actions when it was revealed that he'd just awoken in a mortuary where the local physician/mortician had, moments before, declared him dead.

A 92-year-old man in Paza, Brazil refused to have his wife buried within the four days recommended by the sanitation statutes. His reason? Consuela Roderiguez had already "woken up" from *three* fatal heart attacks and a diabetic coma. In all four instances, she'd been declared dead by qualified doctors. Paolo's faith in his wife was justified once again when, on the fifth day after her "death," Consuela groaned once, coughed twice, opened her eyes and sat up in her coffin. Her comment? "Oh, this box is nice, Papa, so much better than the last one!"

Nor is Scully the first doctor to be startled by a "dead" patient suddenly moving or blinking. Colin Blackmoor, an undertaker from Campbellton, "nearly had heart failure" when Minnie McDermot, brought in dead from a local hospital, "sat up and smacked me right across the face!" as Blackmoor was washing down the body. Ms. McDermot, who had a history of heart disease, had been declared dead twenty-three hours before Blackmoor gave her the "post-mortem" shower that roused her. "She demanded I hand her a sheet off one of the other bodies, went to the phone, called her son, chewed him out royally and then gave him directions to a blue suit she felt would be more appropriate than my sheet for the ride home." Needless to say, Blackmoor is a little less relaxed around his cadavers than he used to be. "Gives a man a fair turn when a thing like that happens."

In Ms. McDermot's case, no autopsy had been performed, or was even planned. She was eighty-three-years-old, with a

Trivia Buster

14

"We've both seen something
like this before."

Special Agent Fox Mulder

Answers

KEEP TRACK OF YOUR TOTAL SCORE.
SEE WHERE YOU'D END UP IN THE
X-FILEAN WORLD OF HIERARCHIES,
SHADOW GOVERNMENTS,
AND CONSPIRACIES.

ONE POINTERS:

1. Mr. Gillnitz's left lung.

2. He tore off his thumb.

3. Albert Tanner or EMT Truelove.

4. "Up to your ass in alligators."

5. Iodine, povidone-iodine to be exact.

TWO POINTERS:

6. Morris.

7. 10.9 pounds.

8. Potassium chloride.

9. 112.

10. Metastatic rhabdomyosarcoma.
    Take 1 point if you said cancer.

YOUR SCORE _____

well-documented history of heart failure, and had "died," in hospital, while under a physician's care. As it was highly unlikely that she was a victim of "foul play," there was really no reason to perform a post-mortem exam. That wasn't the situation in the case of Asuncion Hadle. Ms. Hadle's "death," at a vigorous twenty-three, with no one except a boyfriend with a history of domestic violence in attendance, was considered more than a little suspect. The coroner scheduled to complete the autopsy quickly developed suspicions of his own. Like the fictional Leonard Betts, Asuncion showed none of the usual signs of death. There was no pooling of blood, no stiffness, no discoloration. The only mark on her entire body was a bruise under her hair, just above the nape of her neck. Asuncion Hadle looked as beautiful ten hours after she'd died as she ever had! Victor Ingle, the coroner, even asked that the time of death be checked again. It just didn't seem to match the body before him. When he laid one hand alongside her throat, to start the long Y-incision that would begin the internal portion of the examination, Ingle felt his own heart lurch. Under his thumb was a faint, but distinct, pulse!

"I remember cutting my thumb on the scalpel. I recall calling for one of the tech's. I even remember calling 911." Ingle still shakes his head at the memory. "Then she just opened her eyes. I don't quite recall how it happened, but, well, by the time the EMTs showed up, she was sitting out in my office and I was getting her some coffee. She kept saying how cold she was . . . Well, I guess she was!"

Looking back, the experience is just as disjoint from Asuncion Hadle's point of view. "The last thing I remember was arguing with my boyfriend. I yelled. He got mad. He smacked me and I tumbled back, tripped, and hit my head on something. The next thing I recall is this sweet old man wrapping me up in his coat and feeding me coffee. I stank of disinfectant!"

Fortean Times, a magazine to which several of *The X-Files* crew

NOTEBOOK

Guest Filmography: Paul McCrane

"John Jakes' Heaven & Hell: North & South, Book III" (1994) – Klawdell

The Shawshank Redemption (1994) – Guard Trout

The Portrait (1993) – Bartel

"Cop Rock" (1990) – Det. Bob McIntire

Money, Power, Murder (1989) – Billy Lynn

The Blob (1988) – Deputy Bill Briggs

Robocop (1987) – Emil

"Wiseguy" (1987) – Medley

Hotel New Hampshire (1984) – Frank

Purple Hearts (1984) – Brenner

"Baby Comes Home" (1980) – Bobby Moore

Fame (1980) – Montgomery MacNeil

Rocky II (1979) – Young Patient

X CATCH IT? Betts's escape from the self-storage garage appears to defy several laws of physics. First of all, how exactly did Betts lock a padlock, the same one Mulder unlocked with the spare key, if Betts was *inside* the storage unit? And remember the body that falls out just as Mulder opens the door? How exactly did Leonard's car manage to get out of the unit without running over the body?

NOTEBOOK

Mulder On Evolution

"Recent evolutionary theory would disagree! What scientists call 'punctualism,' or 'punctual equilibrium,' it theorizes that evolutionary changes are cataclysmic, not gradual. That evolution occurs not along a straight graphable line, but in huge fits and starts, and that the unimaginable happens in the gaps – the gap between what we are and what Leonard Betts has become."

When Mulder waxes scientific, most X-Philes remember the chemical impossibilities thrown around in "Firewalker" and just sort of tune out that bit. Occasionally, however, something in one of his 100-word-per-minute spiels actually makes sense! Sort of.

That the various evolutionary theories – yes, there are more than one! – are controversial is no big news. The evolution-creation debate is still hotly contested in forums big and small. But, as the field of evolutionary study, taphonomy, has become more refined, some of these "new" theories seem to jostle Darwin's notions pretty hard. "Seem" is the operative word here, however.

Frankly, anyone reading Darwin's original paper, *The Origin of Species*, would quickly realize that Darwin *never said* that change occurred at a constant rate. He said *natural selection* would be a slow process and, on that count, he seems quite right. Scientists have been assiduously watching for evidence of modern speciation and only on rare occasions have they been lucky enough to actually watch it happen. Darwin also postulated models where "daughter generations" would change so quickly – by means *other* than natural selection – that they'd be unable to interbreed with the "parent generation." Hardly evidence that Darwin believed everything in nature moved at the glacial paces Scully suggested.

In order to say that this Punctuated Equilibria model is "new," it would first be necessary to establish that it contained theories or postulates that had yet to be introduced. When Gould and Eldredge postulated PE as a *mechanism* at work in evolution, they expanded on Darwin's work, they didn't exclude it.

"I mean, wouldn't it make sense that evolution or natural selection would incorporate cancer, the greatest health threat to our species, as part of our genetic makeup?"

Another interesting thought. And one that's actually been proven to work – in some cases. One lab that decided to address the issue of whether organisms could "induce" a specific mutation, one that was not only beneficial, but a response to an immediate problem, is still giving scientists pause for thought.

In the Cairns experiment of 1988, some of the bacteria he exposed to incredibly adverse conditions did adapt, developing a genetic fix for their dilemma. His work left some questions behind, but, it was intriguing enough for another scientist, Hall, to retry the study under more selective experimental conditions. Hall's results were virtual duplicates of Cairns's. Once again, an organism developed a mutation that solved a specific problem.

Transferring that notion to "Leonard Betts" is still something of a stretch, if only because *no* organism has yet developed a mutation to "fix" a *lethal* problem, but this is science fiction, not science, and all science fiction requires is the question "What if . . .?" and an answer somewhere within the realm of extreme possibility. While any number of scientists could prove, without leaving even a shadow of a doubt, that the critters in "Firewalker" weren't changing one element to another, no one can prove, at this time, that mutations to adapt to lethal stimuli aren't possible.

🅧 HMMMM? One can't help wondering where, from a decapitated head, Scully might have obtained the fingerprints she sent to Danny for identification?

CASE CREDITS

WRITTEN BY: Frank Spotnitz, John
   Shiban, and Vince Gilligan
DIRECTED BY: Kim Manners
ORIGINAL PRODUCTION
   NUMBER: 4X14
ORIGINAL US AIRDATE: 01/26/97

GUEST CAST

LEONARD BETTS
   Paul McCrane
MICHELLE WILKES
   Jennifer Clement
EMT
   Lucia Walters
FEMALE EMT
   Laara Sadiq
MALE EMT
   J. Douglas Stewart
NEW PARTNER
   Greg Newmeyer
ELAINE TANNER
   Marjorie Lovett
LOCAL COP
   Sean Campbell
UNIFORMED COP
   Peter Bryant
SECURITY GUARD
   Brad Loree
NIGHT ATTENDANT
   Don Ackerman
PATHOLOGIST
   Dave Hurtubise
DR. CHARLES BURKS
   Bill Dow
BEARDED MAN
   Ken Jones

DEATH TOLL

1 WOMAN: poisoned.
1 MAN: 1 blood loss and chest
   trauma.

are long-time subscribers, reported an equally startling event half-way around the world in southern Taiwan. Mr. Chen Chunnan, who'd apparently died in a car crash in late April, 1996, had been laid out at a funeral home where his heart-broken wife was crying over his body. In between bouts of tears, she wiped her eyes, looked over at her husband and watched as he did a very un-corpse-like thing – he sweated. Needless to say, the funeral planned for the following morning was postponed indefinitely.

For all those miracles, however, there wasn't one for Hi'sin Chin-Lo, who, to all appearances, had been a devoted wife for nearly thirty years. Her one flaw, according to the husband who cut off her head, was that she had bad breath. It was the bad breath that had prompted his impromptu after-dinner decapitation. It seems Mr. Chin, a practicising acupuncturist and herbal physician, had considerable belief in the *chi* and his power to manipulate it. When police arrived at his home, he was leaning over his headless wife, exhorting her to grow a new head. Unlike Betts, Hi'sin Chin-Lo wasn't going anywhere.

Had Scully been a herpetologist instead of a medical doctor, she might have been a bit more wary around Betts's head anyway. While she's right that few of the so-called high animal forms are capable of regenerating, lizards in particular do some very odd things when you separate their heads from their bodies. Though both are technically dead, a lizard's eyes will focus on objects around it for as much as an hour after the decapitation. It'll also bite, flick its tongue, and, in some cases, flush a variety of colors as well. Neat stuff, but disturbing the first time through.

Some episodes mean to "scare the pants off you," some are passion plays in disguise, some are outright tear-jerkers and some, like "Leonard Betts," are a bit of all those things. The good efforts become classics, the less-than-sterling attempts get compared to the last episode to feature regenerating humans, "Forever Young."

CODE NAME:

"Memento Mori"

Case: XF-4X15-02-09-97

CASE SUMMARY

A standard medical examination confirms Leonard Betts's impromptu diagnosis, that Scully has developed a cancerous mass. Mulder's refusal to accept the inevitable, his insistence on tracing the fates of the women Scully met after her abduction, women who, like Scully, are dying of brain tumors, prods her back into action. What she finds, however, seems destined to take her in another direction altogether, a direction diametrically opposed to Mulder's investigations.

CASE HISTORY
More Than A Memory

Titles in *The X-Files* have always served double duty, not just to distinguish one episode from another, but to add another layer of meaning to the on-screen action – while sending curious Philes diving for the expanded versions of their dictionaries. This title, however, may be more confusing than enlightening to viewers without an art history background. Even to those who've heard of the memento moris of previous generations, their particular view of death, and its *relevance*, may still be hard to grasp.

"Memento mori," literally "remember thy death," seemed all too pertinent advice for Scully during this episode – if only for the *hope* it should have inspired. Though the death rites and customs from the times when memento moris were commonplace might seem morbid, bizarre, even macabre to us now, they were meant as much as affirmations of life as they were death tokens and reflected the changing "styles" of death within a community. Their appearance in the middle ages may be related to Christianity's sudden fascination with the "relics" of saints and martyrs, but quickly took on highly individual themes and, by the Victorian era, had progressed well beyond the habit of keeping a locket of hair. No longer were bodies buried somewhere convenient on the family property without so much as a headstone. Deaths, deathbed scenes, and the interment of bodies became highly ritualized events that proscribed the actions of families and communities for considerable stretches of time.

The most familiar of the many types of memento mori have, since the mediaeval era, been items of visual art and, like so many things meant to be symbolic, often appear to hold meanings that modern sensibilities would find completely contradictory to their original intent. How could a death's head, the decoration of a grave marker, become a popular design for a lady's ring? What possible purpose would be served by propping up the recently deceased for a formal photograph? What comfort could reasonably be derived from expending several months' wages to have your dead relative's funerary flowers committed to canvas? Or to building a mausoleum infinitely more expensive than your home?

In one sense, all these seemingly bizarre activities were the ultimate in denial, yet, at their heart, they were also steps in the process of acceptance and an on-going proof that death could be proscribed, that death was still marginally within human control, and that there was indeed a difference between a "good death" and the haphazard, or even accidental, death. Though few of the outward symbols associated with memento moris, no death's heads, no roses held upside down, no morning glories or weeping willows intruded on the scenes, many of the forms and philosophy of the period were present.

For most people, death comes in bed and, in the early nineteenth century for example, it wasn't unusual to confine the ill or infirm to their beds to help them avoid an unseemly end. It's been suggested, with rather strong supporting evidence, that it was the possibility of death inherent in childbirth throughout the mediaeval to Victorian eras that resulted in the woman's "confinement" to a bed instead of being up and walking about, both of which would have made her considerably more comfortable. It may also have satisfied an unstated human impulse to link the beginning of a life with its end.

15

THESE ARE THE EASY ONES! TAKE A SINGLE POINT FOR EACH CORRECT ANSWER.

1. What did Mulder claim to have stolen from a man with a broken leg?

2. Who treated Scully in Allentown?

3. For what condition, besides cancer, were the MUFON women supposedly treated?

4. With whom did Mulder demand that Skinner arrange a meeting?

5. Who helps Mulder break into the Lombard facility?

THESE WILL MAKE YOU THINK, SO GIVE YOURSELF TWO POINTS FOR A CORRECT RESPONSE.

6. What did the realtor scrap off Betsy Hagopian's door?

7. Who was the last member of the original Allentown MUFON group to die?

8. Where did Mulder find the computer password?

9. What did Mulder believe he'd taken from the clones?

10. What combination of therapies did Penny's physician suggest for Scully?

15

Throughout this episode, theories of birth and death are twisted tightly together. The password to a computer list of the dead and dying is hidden in an Easter ornament, itself an example of the life-death-rebirth cycle. The women's deadly cancer is tied to fertility drugs and treatments. As Scully seems prepared to accept her death, Mulder discovers her ova at a facility where the natural order of life is being altered. And, through it all, Scully spends most of her time in bed.

The death-bed scene was once as circumscribed as a wedding ceremony. A full-fledged public ceremony throughout the 12th to 15th centuries, a more private, family occasion up to the end of the Victorian era, the death-bed scene wasn't just a weeping frenzy, it had purpose – to put one's life in order. Those who'd been confined to their beds early had plenty of time to think, to pray, to visit with family, to repair old friendships, to end lingering arguments and to evaluate their lives. For those participating, it was something of an honour to attend a deathbed as it reiterated the importance and esteem in which you were held. The dying gave considerable thought to who they wished to see, and what they would say to them. Advice, guidance, expressions of love, even discussions on philosophy and religion weren't uncommon topics of conversation. In the episode "Memento Mori," Scully's diary fulfills a very similar function for her, as in fact it did in "Dod Kalm." In it she details her advice, her hopes, and her fears about life as well as death. Her visits with and from Penny Northern play out the deathbed scene yet again, and, again, it isn't death that's emphasized, but an evaluation of *life*.

While Scully's confinement isn't as ritualized as those of earlier generations which were so occupied with ensuring that everything that should have been done was done that they created whole books on the etiquette of death, the *ars moriendi,* it evidently fulfilled a need. It was while she was surrounded by death, as out of control and powerless as she's ever been in her own memory, not out chasing down clones and icepickwielding assassins, that she determined there were things she hadn't finished, things she wanted to follow through. The Victorians might not have approved of her decision, you weren't supposed to get off a deathbed after all, but they'd have approved of the *process*. And, in the X-Filean universe, the search is as important as the goal.

The *inability* to attend at a deathbed, a tragedy by mediaeval or Victorian standards, is reflected in this episode as well. Though Scully couldn't call herself Penny's friend, and even denied any memory of a prior relationship, she remained with the other woman until her death, at a time when Scully herself could probably have benefited considerably from undisturbed rest. Perhaps, as her diary entries reflect, she was seeking what others have hoped to find in the deathbed scene – a glimpse into the hereafter, some indication of what her own path would be. It wasn't uncommon for a person's dying words to be captured and remembered by those present, or for transcriptions of the event to be circulated among those unlucky enough not to be in attendance at the time. Even Mulder, though convinced of the importance of his searches elsewhere, returns to her side, to her apparent deathbed, instead of continuing to track his paranormal and pseudo-military sources.

It's not only in these deathbed scenarios that "Memento Mori" holds true to much earlier death customs. Scully's situation, while unique for the present day, has many facets in common with more archaic times. We never learn what steps Mrs. Mulder might have taken if Fox hadn't "risen from the dead on the third day," but Scully's first apparent death, after her abduction by Duane Barry, was played out to the last detail, including the erection of a headstone for her. Even those who pre-arrange their own real-life funerals today haven't quite the intimate knowledge that the fictional Scully does of what her death will mean to those around her. While we may have abandoned many of the philosophical and religious discussions

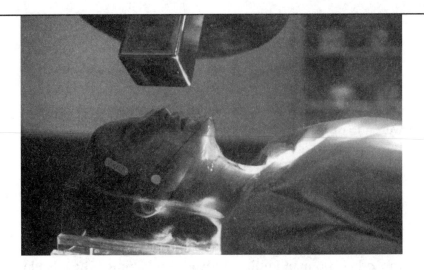

Turn about for Agent Scully as she's the patient instead of the doctor.

common to previous centuries, the maxim to "remember thy death" continues to evoke many levels of meaning. Such contemplations would certainly appeal to Mulder, who remains convinced that her first "death" and this impending crisis are linked in a cause-effect relationship. That her first "death" wasn't nearly as fatal as even her mother would have believed might provide Dana Scully with faith in herself and in the partner who refused to concede her death the first time around, the first person with whom she now chooses to share her illness.

The X-Files has been exploring death, of various sorts, for four years. The first act that Mulder and Scully take on together is the disinterment of a body. Scully's continuous exposure to the technical side of autopsy, instead of just the written reports most agents deal with, is further explored in "Irresistible." The mortality rate among the friends and relatives of both Mulder and Scully has become almost humorous for its frequency, but, in the process, has certainly driven home the mortality of the leads. Mulder held his dying father; Scully buried the sister mistaken for her. Indeed, few episodes haven't included the birth-death-rebirth theme. Mulder rose from the grave of his boxcar. Jeremiah Smith literally brought the dead back to life, Mulder's mother from the brink of death.

From the first season, when Samuel's touch returned life to the dead, and Deep Throat died under Scully's hand, the two have found despair – and hope! – equally surrounded by hope. That both leads have been declared dead already, both separately in "Beyond the Sea" and "Anasazi" and together in "Dod Kalm," only to survive despite the odds, is in itself a source of hope.

"Memento Mori," in satisfying the expectations of the period from which the phrase came, also satisfied the needs of its modern viewers. An argument can even be made that the smaller details, the memento moris themselves, are evolving within this fictional world. Instead of weeping willows, we have snowglobes. Instead of deathbed confessions, we have diaries. The mediaeval mind would have approved.

CASE NOTES
Snowglobes We Have Seen

It seems that *The X-Files* is creating its own eerie series of symbolic objects to accompany the threads of its mythology episodes. Just as a snowglobe provided the life-sustaining gift of water in "Dod Kalm," a snowglobe in "Memento Mori" provided a clue to the life-threatening illnesses of Betsy Hagopian, Penny Northern, Dana Scully and the other women of MUFON. If you were wondering what a "VEGREVILLE" is, and what's it got to do with Easter eggs...

Well, Vegreville, a town of less than 5300 people in the Canadian province of Alberta, claims to own the largest Ukrainian Easter egg, also known as a *pysanka*, in the world. At nine metres high, with 3,512 facets, 6,978 nuts and bolts, 177 internal struts, a 2,000 pound aluminium skin, 3,000 pounds of internal support, and nearly 27,000 pounds of base support, it probably doesn't have much competition.

Pysankas, however, aren't just any old Easter egg. According to legend, the pysanka dates back nearly 6,000 years to the times when Ukrainians were sun worshippers and the eggs,

WRITTEN BY: Chris Carter,
    Frank Spotnitz, John Shiban,
    and Vince Gilligan
DIRECTED BY: Rob Bowman
ORIGINAL PRODUCTION
    NUMBER: 4X15
ORIGINAL US AIRDATE: 02/09/97

GUEST CAST

ASSISTANT DIRECTOR WALTER S.
SKINNER
    Mitch Pileggi
THE CIGARETTE-SMOKING MAN
    William B. Davis
MRS. SCULLY
    Sheila Larken
FROHIKE
    Tom Braidwood
LANGLY
    Dean Haglund
BYERS
    Bruce Harwood
THE GREY-HAIRED MAN
    Morris Panych
PENNY NORTHERN
    Gillian Barber
KURT CRAWFORD
    David Lovgren
DR. KEVIN SCANLON
    Sean Allen
THE WOMAN
    Julie Bond

DEATH TOLL

1 MAN: ice-picked to death
1 WOMAN: of cancer

---

decorated with natural images, commemorated its life-giving properties. When Christianity was brought to the region, Christ's resurrection was tied to the existing spring rituals and the eggs became popular on a wider scale.

In the Ukraine's Carpathian Mountains, the Hutsuls have a completely different take on the purpose of the pysanka. In their folklore, the production of pysankas keeps a powerful snake chained to its rock in the netherworld. As long as the pysankas are made, the world is safe. When the tradition is lost, the snake will break free and devour the world.

Guest Filmography: Gillian Barber

Though *The X-Files* has been criticized for "recycling" the same actors over and over in different roles, it has also been scrupulous in returning the same actor to the same role whenever possible. Amid so many inconsistencies, this little attention to detail provides a more realistic setting against which to display the incredible. It also allows the viewing audience the pleasure of reacquainting themselves with marvellous actors like Gillian Barber.

"The Sentinel" [Red Dust] (1997) – Dr. Gladstone

"The Halfback of Notre Dame" (1996) – Sister Mary Catherine

"In Cold Blood" (1996) – Bonnie Clutter

Jumanji (1996) – Mrs. Thomas

The Outer Limits [The Voice of Reason] (1995) – Fisk

"The Man Who Wouldn't Die" (1995) – Art Hanger-On

"Serving In Silence: The Margarethe Cammermeyer Story" (1995)
    – Col. Koufalis

Double Cross (1994) – Coroner

"Impolite" (1993) – The Voice

"Moment of Truth: A Child Too Many" (1993) – Adoptive Mother

Needful Things (1993) – Myrtle Keeton

A Diagnosis of Murder (1992) – Susan Blankenship

Short Time (1990) – Nurse

Midnight Matinee (1988) – Marilyn

Rainbow War (1985) – Yellow Queen

CODE NAME:

"Unrequited"

Case: XF-4X16-02-23-97

CASE SUMMARY

Mulder and Scully are left rubbing their eyes when a killer targets a group of the military's top brass. Despite the gunman's preference for kills that get up close and personal, no one can see him! One man is killed in the back of his own staff car, another in his empty office. How do you catch a killer that only turns up on video tape?

CASE HISTORY
You Really Can Get What You Deserve

Not only has *The X-Files* enjoyed popular success, it's been lucky enough to have that quality of production noticed and recognized by the industry and industry-watchers. As it begins its fifth season and the first full-length feature film is about to wrap, it seems appropriate to review some of its achievements.

Season One

● For the episode "Darkness Falls," *The X-Files* wins the Environmental Media Award's "Best Drama Series."

● Viewers for Quality Television names *The X-Files* as one of the "best shows on air."

● Following the airing of "Erlenmeyer Flask," the first season finale, the Mystery Writers of America nominated the episode and the series for its Edgar Awards.

● The Canadian Quality Viewers' Coalition named it to its Honor Roll of Exceptional Programs.

● Even in its first season, the program was garnering serious attention, attention reflected in two technical Emmy Award nominations, one for "Best Music for a Title Sequence" and for "Best Title Sequence," which it walked away with. So much for scoffers who thought the germinating bean seeds and static ball effects were too campy!

Season Two

● The Golden Globes hand the program their ultimate honor, "Best Television Drama."

EYEWITNESS STATEMENT

"You might not be able to see him. Isn't it true that US soldiers have reported the unexplained appearance and disappearance of VC guerrillas? I've read the dispatches myself.
I mean, maybe Teager learned something from his captors in twenty-five years of isolation?"

Special Agent Fox Mulder

16

- Entertainment Weekly chooses *The X-Files* as the "Best Television Show of 1994."
- The Viewers for Quality Television repeats its nomination of *The X-Files* for "Best Television Drama" and adds nominations for Gillian Anderson and David Duchovny, personally, as "Best Actress in a Television Drama" and "Best Actor in a Television Drama."
- For the episode "Duane Barry," the American Society of Cinematographers nominates John Bartley for their "Outstanding Achievement Award."
- The Canadian Quality Viewers' Coalition not only nominates *The X-Files* to its Honour Roll once again but, for the first time, names a non-Canadian program as the "Most Innovative Dramatic Series."
- *Television Quarterly* short-lists the program to its "Quality Production List." Every series to make the list has, before ending its original run, received both the Golden Globe and Emmy Awards for Television Drama.
- *The X-Files* is nominated for "Best Drama" by the Television Critics' Association.
- This year's Emmy Awards nominations list is considerably longer than the previous year. Among them:
  - Outstanding Drama Series
  - Outstanding Individual Achievement, Writing–Drama: *Chris Carter for "Duane Barry."*
  - Outstanding Cinematography, Series: *John Bartley for "One Breath."*
  - Outstanding Individual Achievement in Editing / Single Camera Production:
  James Coblenz for "Duane Barry", Stephen Mark for "Sleepless."
  - Outstanding Sound Editing:
  Series Sound Editor: *Thierry Couturier;*
  Sound Effects Editors: *Stuart Calderson, Chris Fradkin, Michael Kimball, David Van Slyke, Susan Welsh, and Matt West;*

THESE ARE THE EASY ONES! TAKE A SINGLE POINT FOR EACH CORRECT ANSWER.

1. What was left on the victims?

2. What was the name of the group the FBI targeted for surveillance?

3. What monument was to be rededicated?

4. How many men were on Teager's list?

5. What did Teager give Danzinger at the ceremony?

THESE WILL MAKE YOU THINK, SO GIVE YOURSELF TWO POINTS FOR A CORRECT RESPONSE.

6. Nathaniel Teager was a member of the Green Beret detachment B-11, who were also known as . . . ?

7. What religion was POW Gary Davenport?

8. Who signed off on Nathaniel Teager's death certificate?

9. Who was driving the first victim?

10. What was Teager's service number?

Answers

KEEP TRACK OF YOUR TOTAL SCORE.
SEE WHERE YOU'D END UP IN THE
X-FILEAN WORLD OF HIERARCHIES,
SHADOW GOVERNMENTS,
AND CONSPIRACIES.

<u>ONE POINTERS:</u>

1. A playing card with a death's head on the obverse side.

2. The Right Hand.

3. The Wall, the Vietnam Veterans' Memorial.

4. 3.

5. A list of POWs.

<u>TWO POINTERS:</u>

6. The Bloody Sabers.

7. Catholic.

8. General Steffan.

9. Private Burkholder.

10. 82278.

YOUR SCORE _____

Music Editor: *Jeff Charbonneau;* ADR Editor: *Debby Ruby Winsberg;*
Dialogue Editors: *Machiek Malish and Chris Reeves for "Duane Barry."*
♦ Outstanding Guest Actress, Drama:
C. C. H. Pounder for "Duane Barry" (Agent Kazdin).

Season Three

● The Golden Globes nominates both leads for their roles: David Duchovny for "Best Actor, Drama" and Gillian Anderson for "Best Actress, Drama."

● The pair receive the same nominations from their own union, the Screen Actors' Guild, David Duchovny for "Best Actor, Drama" and Gillian Anderson for "Best Actress, Drama," which she wins – to her evident surprise and her fans' delight.

● Making it a three-peat, the Viewers for Quality Television once again nominates *The X-Files* for "Best Television Series, Drama."

● The Speculative Fiction Association of the Americas awards *The X-Files* its "Best Television Series, Drama" prize, beating out *The Outer Limits*, a strong favorite, in the process.

● Chris Carter's union, the Directors' Guild of America, honors him with a nomination for "Best Direction of a Television Series, Drama" for "The List."

● The Producers' Guild of America nominates *The X-Files* for "Best Television Drama."

● The Emmy Awards is justifiably generous with its nominations – and awards – this year:
♦ Outstanding Individual Achievement – Writing, Drama: *Darin Morgan wins for "Clyde Bruckman's Final Repose."*
♦ Outstanding Achievement – Cinematography: *John S. Bartley wins for "Grotesque."*

- Outstanding Achievement – Sound Editing: *"Nisei" wins.*
- Outstanding Achievement – Sound Mixing: *"Nisei" wins again!*
- Outstanding Guest Actor, Drama: *Peter Boyle wins for "Clyde Bruckman's Final Repose."*
- Outstanding Drama Series
- Outstanding Lead Actress, Drama: *Gillian Anderson*
- Outstanding Achievement, Art Direction: *Graeme Murray* and Shirley Inget for "Jose Chung's From Outer Space"

Season Four

- Once again, the Golden Globes is good to *The X-Files*'s staff. This time around, the top spots were all going to the same table.
- Best Television Drama: *The X-Files wins.*
- Best Actress in a Dramatic Television Role: *Gillian Anderson wins.*
- Best Actor in a Dramatic Television Role: *David Duchovny wins, completing the sweep.*
- The Canadian League of Concerned Viewers, whose awards always go to those programs and roles it feels best demonstrate personal strength and personal value, award *The X-Files* and Gillian Anderson their top accolades.
- The Screen Actors' Guild remains enchanted with *The X-Files*, nominating it for four awards: *Best Series – Drama, Best Actress in a Dramatic Television Role, Best Actor in a Dramatic Television Role, and even Best Ensemble Cast for a Television Drama. And, once again, Gillian Anderson walks away with the prize.*
- The Viewers for Quality Television obviously continues its approbation, nominating *The X-Files* for the fourth time as "Best Quality Drama," the leads for "Best Actor in a Quality Drama" and "Best Actress in a Quality Drama," and Mitch Pileggi for "Best Recurring Player in a Quality Drama."

The dress that provoked so many 'golden globe' jokes.

X CATCH IT? There was a special thanks to Jan Scruggs of the Vietnam Veterans' Memorial Fund at the end of this episode.

CASE NOTES
Under The Flag

The X-Files has no taboos. There are no sacred cows.

There are things it steps warily around, but there are no topics, agencies, or even individuals it won't tackle. Religions, organized or not, have been engaged with on a regular basis. There was Samuel the tent-hopping miracle worker, whose "father" fit all the stereotypes but who himself was what might be least expected in that setting – the real McCoy. In "Revelations," Scully's Catholic-school upbringing is resurrected by an incorruptible corpse and a young boy who may be the only true miracle in a series of fraudulent claims. "Kaddish" dragged viewers into the world of Judaic mysticism and left them wondering where the reality ended and fiction took over.

Sex, the other great taboo, merits no lack of attention either. In episodes as early as "GenderBender" and as recent as "Never Again," Scully's sex life – or lack thereof – has been

"Unrequited" lets us see our Dynamic Duo in a more classic FBI profile.

an open book. Mulder's "video library" and his discount account with the local phone sex firm are, by now, standing jokes. We've even pried into Skinner's sex life – unsuccessful though it might be! Even the fact that Mulder's one serious encounter with the opposite sex happened to be a woman with a liking for the Gothic scene who believed she was a vampire seems somehow appropriate and, if not normal, then completely non-startling.

With sex and religion accounted for, we come to pop idols and quickly discover there's no room for idolatry in the *X-File*an world. In fact, some few modern-day icons seem singled out for continuing derision: "Oh, so he's a killer and a golfer," and "Do the words 'Orenthal James Simpson' mean anything to you?" just sort of spring to mind, as do the half-dozen or so references to Elvis Presley.

But it's when the military, regardless of branch, gets added to the conspiracy mix that the taboo gloves really come off. Perhaps it's a natural consequence of building your series on the assumption that "something" landed in Roswell, something the military not only covered up but also used for their own purposes, that makes all things military easy targets, but *The X-Files* has certainly been "setting 'em up and knocking 'em down" since the beginning.

In "Deep Throat," the second episode of the first season, Scully ends up rescuing her partner from a military base that appears fully equipped to either recycle UFO parts or erase selected sections of human memory. Definitely not nice people.

"Space," which portrayed Mulder as the overawed space cadet wannabe, seemed ready to single out a certain slice of the military, test pilots, as being a little bit above the common sludge, even ending with the noble sacrifice of Colonel Belt, but despite that the episode left a wide smear across the reputation of military/space history.

You know you've made it when you've been spoofed by Mad Magazine, Saturday Night Live, and . . . (drumroll, please) your own station's adult cartoon!

CASE CREDITS

WRITTEN BY: Howard Gordon,
  Chris Carter
DIRECTED BY: Michael Lange
ORIGINAL PRODUCTION
  NUMBER: 4X16
ORIGINAL US AIRDATE: 02/23/97

GUEST CAST

ASSISTANT DIRECTOR WALTER
S. SKINNER
  Mitch Pileggi
NATHANIEL TEAGER
  Peter LaCroix
GENERAL BENJAMIN BLOCH
  Scott Hylands
LIEUTENANT GENERAL PETER
MACDOUGAL
  Bill Agnew
GENERAL JON STEFFAN
  William Nunn
GENERAL LEITCH
  William Taylor
PFC GUS BURKHOLDER
  Don McWilliams
FEMALE PRIVATE
  Jen Jasey
AGENT CAMERON HILL
  Ryan Michael
AGENT EUGENE CHANDLER
  Mark Holden
DENNY MARKHAM
  Larry Musser
RENEE DAVENPORT
  Lesley Ewen
DR. BEN KEYSER
  Allan Franz

DEATH TOLL

2 MEN: shot at close range

136

In any number of episodes to follow, the military became a convenient "bad guy" for Mulder to bang his head against, for army-brat Scully to cautiously support and to conveniently dispose of any evidence that might actually be discovered. "Fallen Angel" not only presented the military as a committed alien-hunter, but an organization completely unconcerned with the welfare of its own members. Season two opened with "Little Green Men" and a covert military unit that chased Mulder over half of Puerto Rico, mostly off-road, while shooting at two of the supposedly unarmed citizens the standing American army is supposed to be busy defending. "Fresh Bones", which set up the military as a sort of large-scale babysitting agency that someone really should have used the Nanny-cam on, gave us two different views of the army, depending on how many stripes or stars an individual soldier might have: The more stars, the more likely any given character was to be a cold-hearted, ruthless power monger; the fewer stripes, the more likely any given enlisted man was to be either perennially stupid or dead. Neither characterization did much for the military's press image.

"Unrequited," at least thematically, continued developing a fairly consistent X-Filean point of view, namely that big institutions are Bad Things, likely to do More Bad Things to the American public or its own soldiers. "Sleepless," which gave us a surgically altered unit whose leader was now on the rampage in an attempt to destroy not only the people who'd created and abandoned the unit but his fellow soldiers as well, was, plotwise, little different from "Unrequited." Likewise, "The Walk" went over the same ground yet again, changing little but the paranormal twist of the week.

Given the number of military-oriented episodes The X-Files has brought off so far, it seems likely it'll continue to set 'em up and knock 'em down, creating the occasional sympathetic character like Nathaniel Teager whose sole purpose will be to point out just how nasty everyone else in uniform must be.

CODE NAME:

"Tempus Fugit"

CASE SUMMARY

Mulder and Scully are shocked to discover that the victims of a commercial airline crash included well-known alien abductee Max Fenig – and that Fenig had predicted the crash. When investigators begin turning up anomalous evidence, including the suspicious absence of any wristwatches among the bodies, Mulder starts to suspect that Flight 549 wasn't the only "aircraft" in the sky that night.

CASE HISTORY
"I Know You Won't Believe Me . . ."

That's the opening line Dr. Lynn Hauser has heard over five hundred times since deciding to turn her general practise psychiatry offices into a special clinic for those who sincerely believe they're victims of alien abductions, assaults and even rapes.

"It's difficult for the general public to understand the stress levels these patients live with. If I could compare it to anything, it would probably be to the Post-Traumatic Stress Syndrome most often encountered in war veterans, especially those who returned from active tours of duty to discover folks back home had a vastly different view of the war than they did."

The group of patients meeting in the conference room for their weekly encounter session all have one thing in common – they look perfectly normal.

"My patients aren't crazy, they don't go around like that chess player with tin foil wrapped around his head to keep out the 'voices.' Most of them live what we might call 'perfectly adjusted' lives, with the small exception that they believe they were kidnapped by something alien."

Carla G., an accounting clerk and mother of two, certainly wouldn't draw any attention in an elevator, but, according to Dr. Hauser, is the highest rate "repeater" in the group. "She recalls incidents that go well back into her childhood, some

EYEWITNESS STATEMENT

"You want to know what I think, Scully? I'm going to tell you. I think Max was abducted, sucked right out of this door at 29,000 feet. The burns we're seeing are the result of that abduction, and all the evidence here will point to that conclusion, but it will be dismissed because of its improbability, its unthinkability. The crash of Flight 549 will go unsolved – unless we find a way to prove it."

Special Agent Fox Mulder

memories are tied to events we know to have taken place when she was only four or five years old."

What sort of "incidents?"

"Fairly classic abduction scenarios: a feeling of paralyzation, bright lights, blackouts, pain, some vague memories of short figures poking her frozen form with long fingers, more pain, more blackness, then the realization that she was not where she went to sleep."

It might easily be put down to childhood nightmares, if particularly vivid ones, except that Carla's story is one of the very few that have some, admittedly slight, corroborating evidence. Also present for the meeting is Carla's mother, a slight woman with gray hair, gray eyes, and hands that move restlessly in her lap as she looks around the room. "It's true that we used to find Carla in all kinds of strange places. At least half a dozen times I thought I'd have to call the police, but each time we'd find her before we had to do that. We figured she was sleepwalking, I did that myself when I was a child. Still, after the first few times, we became pretty conscious of which doors in the house were open or unlocked, and once she was settled in for the night I got into the habit of latching up everything, even though we lived in one of those sorta languid Southern towns where nothing much happened, certainly nothing dangerous enough to set people to locking their doors at eight o'clock in the evening. Still, she must have found a way because once, when I knew I'd locked everything up, I peeked in to check on her and found her bed empty. I called her dad at work and he came home to help look for her. We discovered her curled up asleep next to the motor for the pool's plastic cover. Neither her dad nor I could see how she got out in the first place." A pucker develops between the gray eyebrows as her eyes sweep the room again. "We certainly wouldn't have ever thought of something like this!"

Trivia Buster

17

THESE ARE THE EASY ONES! TAKE A SINGLE POINT FOR EACH CORRECT ANSWER.

1. What was unusual about one passenger's sidearm?

2. What did Mulder give Scully for her birthday?

3. What time did all the crash victims' watches read?

4. In which row were Max Fenig and his chatty seatmate sitting?

5. What did Mulder find in Max Fenig's pocket?

THESE WILL MAKE YOU THINK, SO GIVE YOURSELF TWO POINTS FOR A CORRECT RESPONSE.

6. What was Max Fenig's flight number?

7. What items did the team leader promise Mulder he'd keep an eye out for?

8. How many people, passengers and crew, were supposed to be on the plane?

9. What alias was Max Fenig using?

10. From what hotel did Max Fenig's sister, Sharon Graffia, disappear?

Answers

KEEP TRACK OF YOUR TOTAL SCORE. SEE WHERE YOU'D END UP IN THE X-FILEAN WORLD OF HIERARCHIES, SHADOW GOVERNMENTS, AND CONSPIRACIES.

ONE POINTERS:

1. It was made of plastic.

2. An Apollo 11 keychain.

3. 8:01.

4. Unlucky 13, D and F to be exact.

5. Mulder's FBI business card.

TWO POINTERS:

6. Flight 549.

7. Green alien goo and Dr. Spock's phaser.

8. 134.

9. Paul Gidney.

10. The Paradise Motel.

YOUR SCORE _____

The rest of the group arrive promptly, none of them sporting clothes with bizarre slogans or green hair or anything else out of the ordinary. In total, twelve patients have joined the discussion this evening. Two are auto mechanics, two are confidential secretaries with highly responsible and independent positions, one is a doctor, three work at a local canning operation, one is a priest. They sit quietly, attentive to one another's questions and comments. Occasionally, some item will start a round of nodding as they all seem to relate to a particular detail in the narration. When Dr. Hauser suggests some psychological models that might begin to explain their experiences in less exotic ways, the possibility that naturally occurring apnea might account for the "light at the end of the tunnel" effect, all twelve appear anxious to give her theories serious consideration. A hand rises slowly at the back of the room and Tina B. leans forward.

"I can see what you're suggesting, something similar to a near-death experience, but do you think a person could stop breathing long enough to have an experience like that and still be wide awake?" Dr. Hauser looks at her curiously and waits as she continues. "I mean, the first time I can remember being . . . taken away, I was sitting in my car, wide awake, trying to find the gas bill!" Like several members of this group, Tina B. is what's known as a repeater. Like the fictional Max Fenig, she believes she's been abducted not once, but many times. Unlike Carla, Tina had a perfectly normal childhood and was twenty-three when her life "was turned on its head" and she "stopped being sure things were exactly as they appeared." Her question is thoughtful, almost hopeful, but there aren't any firm answers for her tonight.

Dr. Hauser makes a note on her pad before answering. "I doubt a waking person would suffer from apnea at all, but that's not necessarily true. I can invite a sleep specialist to come in and discuss the pathology involved, or, if you prefer

I can make individual referrals." Someone quickly opts for the private referral and several of the group follow the lead. Dr. Hauser's pencil is flying across her note pad. After the meeting, she explains that because so many abduction scenarios occur at night, some psychologists believe the answer to these people's profound belief in alien abduction lies in their sleep habits. "We've all experienced vivid dreams from time to time, the ones that make you get out of bed and turn on the lights. Some sleep disorders can actually intensify the dreaming process, making it seem as real as any waking experience. If you were to combine that condition with something like apnea, it's possible that the result would be the 'alien abduction' experience."

So Dr. Hauser herself doesn't believe in the literal truth of her patients' stories?

A long pause follows.

"When I started interviewing abductees, I was certain that some common pathology, some common experience, would make itself evident during the course of treatments. I wasn't the type of person to believe in UFOs and aliens, I'm still not. What I am, though, is thoroughly impressed by the consistencies I hear in these people's statements. It was just that quality that attracted me to the phenomenon, but I hadn't realized what a compelling picture their stories would present me with. It's not the big things that catch you, you expect that, the whole 'bright place' experience is actually common in a few other fields of investigation as well. It's the details. One of the first women who came to the clinic, a Joanne G., related a rather precise event from one of her experiences. She told me about a cramp developing in her leg because she was just a tad taller than the table she'd been laid on. The cold metal edge pressing into her calf gave her a vicious charlie-horse. Then she told me how one of the 'aliens' had massaged the cramp away with a warm cloth that seemed almost like a tiny electric blanket. Just two months ago, a male subject presented with an identical story, except the cramp was an inch or so above the back of his knee, a location consistent with Joanne's if you make an allowance for height differences." Her chuckle seems a little strained. "On days like that, I really wonder if our psyches can possibly be that primed for identical dream experiences, or, if, maybe, the simplest solution to the whole abductee phenomenon isn't that their experiences are all the same because they're all true . . ." She looks up again. "But that's only on a very few days. Most of the time I feel like I'm just inches from discovering some logical way of putting it all together, of finding a real, tangible, scientific reason why some four hundred people each year have experiences like these."

Back in her office, more questions come to mind. "Don't sessions like yours, which gather people with questionable experiences together, only serve to reinforce their beliefs?"

"Not really. You meet them, and what they, and most people in their situation, are looking for isn't confirmation that they were abducted. They're trying to understand what mechanism other than that might account for their memories. For example, several years ago, I took one group through an exercise designed to explain the 'false memory' syndrome and how it might apply to their own problem."

"And how do you go about proving there are such things as 'false memories'? Isn't it inherently more difficult to disprove a negative statement than a positive one?"

"Yes and no. Human beings make models, mental constructs to help them store and retrieve information. When I was little, I learned rhymes and songs to help me remember how to spell

'Mississippi' and 'arithmetic.' As an adult, I still tend to learn concepts, not details. For example, I can figure out that the hypotenuse of a triangle with one short side of three feet and a long side of four feet is five feet. I don't have to specifically remember the 3,4,5-foot ratio because I can deduce it.

"Here, listen to this list of words and try to remember them: recollect, recall, recognize, place, identify. Now repeat them back to me."

I do, to the best of my ability. "Recall, recognize, identify, remember—"

She shakes her head. "The word 'remember' wasn't in the list, it was part of the instructions. But because it seemed to fit with the general category of words I gave you, in fact might be considered a 'logical' member of that group of words, your mind made it part of the list you 'remembered.' The important point is that I never even said I was giving you a list of related words, that's an assumption you naturally began to make when you saw what appeared to be a pattern. Our brains love patterns. If you want to try the same test on someone else, just assemble a list of words based on a single idea but don't include the word you used as your base. In up to eighty percent of the cases you test, you'll find the subject includes the word anyway – and will swear they heard you say it!"

It's certainly a neat trick, and probably a good way to pick up some cash at the local pub, but how do these mental games apply to alien abductees?

"In the absence of physical proof that aliens are 'borrowing' human beings, the only evidence that abductions might be happening at all is in the memories of the abductees. It's that sense of conviction, their complete confidence in their own memories, that often prevents them from accepting even the possibility that what they remember might not have happened exactly as they recall. In my opinion, my job as a therapist

X BLOOPER! The plane that Scully was waiting for had N9747P as its registration number, but the plane Mulder later chases down is C-FHTC. That's a Canadian designation, not likely to be involved in any rescue activities so far south of the border.

143

isn't to decide if what they believe happened to them was objectively real. My job is to help them function in the real world.

"If I was treating Carla for arachnophobia, for example, I'd have two ways to approach the problem. I could take the position that her fear stemmed from some incident or incidents, something she might or might not actually remember or even associate with her fear of spiders, and try to eliminate the root of her fear. Or I might just accept that the fear exists and help her find ways to cope with it. The choice of approach and treatment would depend on a number of factors including the patient's stated objective and the style of therapy I practised."

So are the majority of your patients looking for affirmation that what they experienced was real? Or are they just trying to cope with the 'experience' and move on?

"Most are, I think, looking for a good reason to doubt themselves."

That sounds rather sad.

"In a sense, it is. No therapist would suggest a patient simply attempt to amputate an 'experience' that has undoubtedly shaped a considerable proportion of their views and beliefs. What we're trying to do here is integrate those memories and give these patients a way to cope on a day to day basis. Remember those Vietnam vets I was talking about? Well, I can't make the war un-happen for them. What I can do is help them deal with the disorientation they feel because of the different perspective they bring to the rest of their lives, give them coping mechanisms that allow them to relate, and a place where they can discuss their problems with people who understand."

More of those "through the window" effects!

If Max Fenig were a real person and he were to walk in here tomorrow, what would you do for him? What could you do for him?

"In all honesty, not much. There is a certain percentage of abductees who can't just cope. Like the man in your tape, they're driven to find explanations for what happened to them – or what they believe happened. What they're looking for isn't affirmation – they know, they don't need me or you to agree with them. They aren't trying to make their perspective match in with the rest of those around them. They're looking for something solid, something they can point to and say, without doubt, 'There is the proof.' "

What if that proves impossible? Do these driven individuals eventually give up?

"Not in my experience."

So what happens to them?

"Well, let me give you another scenario. Suppose you're a ten-year-old boy who has just gotten his first puppy. You know

CASE CREDITS

WRITTEN BY: Chris Carter and
   Frank Spotnitz
DIRECTED BY: Rob Bowman
ORIGINAL PRODUCTION
   NUMBER: 4X17
ORIGINAL US AIRDATE: 03/16/97

GUEST CAST

AGENT PENDRELL
   Brendan Beiser
MAX FENIG
   Scott Bellis
MIKE MILLAR
   Joe Spano
CORPORAL FRISH
   Tom O'Brien
SERGEANT ARMANDO GONZALES
   Rick Dobran
THE FATHER
   Jon Raitt
THE INVESTIGATOR
   Marek Wiedman
THE PILOT
   Mark Wilson
SHARON GRAFFIA
   Chilton Crane
SCOTT GARRETT
   Greg Michaels
BRUCE BEARFIELD
   Robert Moloney
LAROLD REBHUN
   Jerry Schram
MOTEL MANAGER
   Felicia Schulman
DARK MAN
   David Pálffy

DEATH TOLL

133 MEN, WOMEN AND CHILDREN:
   unknown causes concomittant
   with a plane crash and/or
   radiation burns
2 MEN: 1 apparently self-inflicted
   gun-shot wound to the head,
   1 shot to death
1 WOMAN: shot to death

you're responsible for his care and, in general, you're diligent in your chores. Then one night, as you fall asleep, you realize you forgot to put down fresh water before going to bed. That's real, a fact. You drift off anyway and dream that your dog died. You wake up with your heart pounding, tears running down your face and a very real sense of horror and grief. Your body responds as if the dog had really died and so, to a great extent, does your heart and your mind. You race downstairs and water the dog. Now, tell me, does it really matter if the dream was a dream? Your actions from that point on are likely to reflect the fact that you've learned what a responsibility it is to be the one caring for that helpless puppy. The dog didn't actually have to die for you to learn from the experience. It didn't have to die to change your view of the world or how you react to that world. That's why I don't try to judge how 'real' my patients' experiences have been, and why some of them will never be able to believe they weren't abducted."

CASE NOTES
Guest Filmography: Scott Bellis

If X-Philes had been polled to determine which of the many wonderful guest stars featured in *The X-Files*'s first seventy episodes they'd most like to have reprise their role, Scott Bellis might well have topped the list. Though the crew at 10-13 apparently didn't see any need to explain just where Max has been since he disappeared from that warehouse two years ago, fans were willing to overlook that little continuity issue in the interest of a story as riveting as the "Tempest Fugit / Max" two-parter. Of course, they'd probably have preferred he remain alive . . .

"The Man Who Wouldn't Die" (1995) – Boris

Inspection (1994) – Van Driver

Little Women (1994) – John McCracken

Timecop (1994) – Ricky

"MacGyver" [There But For The Grace] (1991) – Danny

CODE NAME:

"Max"

Case: XF-4X18-03-23-97

EYEWITNESS STATEMENT

"Men with Spartan lives, simple in their creature comforts, if only to allow for the complexity of their passions."

Special Agent Dana Scully, on Fox Mulder and Max Fenig

CASE SUMMARY

Max Fenig is dead, but questions remain. Why did his flight fall out of the sky? What was he carrying that left radioactive burns on both him and his seatmate? Why was a military air-traffic controller asked to lie? Why is that controller's duty partner dead? And, perhaps most important of all, what happened in the nine minutes that are still unaccounted for?

CASE HISTORY
Coming and Going

Max Fenig, according to Mulder's interpretation of events, was plucked from the pressure-sealed cabin of a full-size commercial airliner that just happened to be travelling at 30,000 feet. Believe it or not, that's not even considered all that unusual a scenario by any number of UFO investigators, who claim that some thousand people are taken and given back each year – many under equally outrageous conditions!

Larry Poerter reports the bizarre case of a Cincinnati man who'd actually moved to the urban centre in a bid to avoid alien notice. As he suspected he'd already been temporarily removed from his Ohio farmstead several times, Clinton Baker was hoping he'd go a little more unnoticed with more neighbours close by. It doesn't seem to have worked. On May 12, 1996, Baker contacted Poerter, who'd taken his previous abduction reports, from a gas station phone booth on the outskirts of one of Cincinnati's "bedroom" suburbs. Poerter, after getting an address from his highly agitated acquaintance, headed for the phone booth and discovered Baker, completely naked and covered in red mud, crouching in the bottom of the glass unit. While delivering Baker back to his new apartment, some three miles distant, Poerter prodded him for an account of his actions that evening and was told, "I ran the tub and was just about to get in when I woke up with a blinding headache in the phone booth." Poerter was the only person Baker knew in Cincinnati and the first person he'd called.

Back in Baker's new apartment, Poerter discovered a bathtub full of water that had already cooled to room temperature and a pile of discarded clothes, but no sign of an alien invasion. While it's possible that a 6' 3" naked man could walk the three miles from the apartment building to the phone booth, and it's possible that he could do it without being noticed, and it's possible that he could have left his security building without setting off an alarm on the side door, one thing is guaranteed – according to the building's lobby camera, not a single naked man, or a clothed Clinton Baker for that matter, passed out through after he arrived home from a grocery expedition at three o'clock that afternoon.

When Lainie Crane of Seattle awoke from a "dream" peopled with height-impaired green men, she was even more startled to discover she'd been lying on the roof of her new bungalow, in February, long enough to accumulate a light dusting of snow over her pajamas. Afraid not only of heights, but of the very real possibility of sliding off the roof of her house, Ms Crane decided that shouting for help, as opposed to skittering across the expanse of slippery shingles, was the better part of valor and set up a commotion loud enough to awaken her next door neighbor in fairly short order. Perhaps not surprisingly, Lainie Crane wasn't paying much attention to snow tracks as she was helped, shivering, off her roof, but her neighbor wasted no time in asking just how she'd managed to get up there without leaving any tracks anywhere around the house. Putting it down to sleepwalking and enough snow to cover whatever tracks she might have made in her nocturnal wanderings, an embarrassed Ms Crane thanked her neighbor and retreated to the warmth of her house.

It was only in the morning that she realized that none of her windows opened onto the roof, that there wasn't so much as a trellis or tree that could have given her access to the roof and – most importantly – that she didn't own a ladder! Her neighbor had brought his own on his rescue call.

Answers

KEEP TRACK OF YOUR TOTAL SCORE.
SEE WHERE YOU'D END UP IN THE
X-FILEAN WORLD OF HIERARCHIES,
SHADOW GOVERNMENTS,
AND CONSPIRACIES.

ONE POINTERS:

1. An Airstream trailer.

2. NICAP.

3. A whopper.

4. 3.

5. A "Tickle-Me Elmo."

TWO POINTERS:

6. An F-15 Eagle.

7. Soul Coughing's
"Unmarked Helicopters."

8. (202)-555-2350

9. SYR, for Syracuse, NY.

10. Cummins Aerospace.

YOUR SCORE _____

The long-distance winner, however, is undoubtedly Robert Askin. Mr. Askin left his Boston offices at his usual time, 6:05, on a Friday evening and headed off down the coast to meet his family at their summer home on Cape Cod for the weekend. He didn't arrive and his wife quickly notified the police. When he was found at 3:35 a.m., without the car that would later turn up in Oklahoma, he was in Buffalo! While it's possible to drive that distance in the time available to him, police were naturally confused as to how he'd managed to ditch the car several states away and still arrive in Buffalo the following morning. Suggestions that Askin had been intent on deserting his wife and children, and that an accomplice had taken the car to confuse the trail, just didn't pan out. Askin had been seen, still in his car, just outside Hyannisport by a gas-pump attendant who knew the man well. A credit card receipt confirmed the time and location, making it almost impossible for him to even get to Buffalo, much less make secret tryst with accomplices along the way.

For his part, Robert Askin maintains that he has no memory of anything between the gas station and the street where he was found wandering in Buffalo.

Most people who awaken with dim memories of another place, a place with a "bright light," find themselves exactly where they were to begin with and with little more than a vague sense of having lost time between one action and the next. Alicia Taylor reported just such an incident to her local UFO chapter, but her story had a twist. A complete technophobe, Alicia was the classic can't-even-set-the-VCR type. In fact, that's exactly what she was doing when she "lost time." She clearly remembers looking at her wristwatch, noting the time as 10:22 p.m., and then looking up to adjust the time on her VCR. It was still blinking that annoying 12:00 when she suddenly found herself just staring at the machine. Looking back down to her watch to continue to set the clock, she was shocked to see it was now 12:12. A quick glance at the television confirmed that the evening news, which had been airing when she started the whole process, had been over for some time.

Thinking she might have had some sort of seizure, which might also explain the horrid taste in her mouth, Ms Taylor made an appointment with her doctor for the following day, but despite a battery of unpleasant tests no medical explanation for the missing hour and fifty minutes was found.

Conception Guierrez never actually noticed her "blank times" until one evening, when she thought she was home helping her daughter with her homework, she discovered herself walking along a street two blocks away. The realization that she wasn't where she was supposed to be was so startling and disorienting that she spun about on her heel to race home and immediately stepped out in front of a car. In addition to Conception's statement, which the recording officer noted seemed "muddled," was the equally unusual sworn testimony of the driver. He didn't claim that he simply "didn't see her" as hundreds of drivers in similar situations have done, he claimed "she wasn't there!" According to the police report, there were no cars parked along the street to impair the driver's view. This was a new housing area and, consequently, there were no tree-lined avenues that might create visual blocks. Though no one believed either of them, and there was no evidence to contradict their stories, one thing remains true – the only two eye-witnesses to the event, Conception and the driver, both agree she "just appeared" on the sidewalk. When questioned, Conception's daughter, who'd just started kindergarten that year, reportedly said, "She just disappeared, so I went to bed." Conception's sense of other-worldliness only increased when her bemused husband confirmed the fact that his wife had been disappearing at odd intervals "ever since we were married." Why hadn't he said anything? "Because, well, because I love her, and if she wasn't ready to talk about it, I wasn't going

X Several of the writers associated with *The X-Files* are Hitchcock fans so they'd immediately recognize that it didn't really matter what was in the box. Hitchcock called such items McGuffins. No one cared what the McGuffin was, it was enough that somebody wanted it.

to force her." Conception Guierrez is probably the only wife on the planet who could wish for a slightly less understanding husband!

Most abductees, even fictional ones like the adorable Max Fenig, however, are all too aware of their disappearances. Tyrell Cobb could certainly identify with the character. He, too, believes he's been taken dozens of times, and his memory of several of those occasions is all too clear. In 1987 he checked himself into a mental institution, and asked them to watch him while he slept, to "make sure he was there the whole time." While voluntary inmates are usually allowed considerably more freedom than other patients, something about Tyrell Cobb made at least one of his doctors uncomfortable enough to have him assigned to one of the "suicide watch" rooms which was equipped with closed-circuit cameras that recorded the activity within the room for an eight-hour stretch and fed a live image back to a nurse's station. A wall of glass also provided staff with firsthand images of anything happening in the rooms and Tyrell Cobb had no objection to leaving the privacy curtains wide open. After what he called his "first decent night's sleep" in two years, Cobb sat down with two psychiatrists and proceeded to tell them his story. Though he had no physical proof, he claimed to have been the subject of numerous alien

Mulder's last moments with Max Fenig in the episode "Fallen Angel."

152

experiments, that he'd been subjected to mind-numbing drugs which resulted in his losing days from his memory and that he was sure "they" would be back to finish the job.

Needless to say, he was immediately tested for a number of drugs, mind-numbing and otherwise. Though – on the down side for Cobb – the tests failed to turn up any unusual chemicals in his system, they also proved he wasn't some whacked-out addict who'd imagined the whole thing in a drugged stupor. He remained at the hospital for eight days, and though he never physically disappeared he registered some highly unusual readings on two separate EEG scans. Further investigation into those results revealed "no underlying causality." In other words, no one could explain the smooth brain wave patterns Cobb registered for periods as long as thirty-two minutes at a time. And it looks like Cobb will continue to be something of a mystery. When he checked himself out on the eighth day he reported back to his job at a local hotel, completed his shift, walked out the front door and disappeared. No one has seen him since November of 1987.

CASE NOTES
Rest In Peace

When Chris Carter made the decision to kill off Deep Throat in the first season, fans were shocked. Killing off a recurring character just wasn't done, at least not permanently, and though Jerry Hardin has reprised the role in several episodes, as a dead man, the latest in a series of morphs, and in flashbacks, the fact remains that he's dead – very dead. At the time, Carter said he'd wanted to make the point that *The X-Files* wasn't ordinary television, that anything could – and would – be expected to happen at any time. Fans quickly added the caveat "and especially around Sweeps Weeks."

Since then, a number of seemingly intrinsic characters have been rather casually wiped from the players' list. We'd just been

X HMMM? Max must be on some sort of alien abduction mailing list. When he first appeared in "Fallen Angel," he was tracking an invisible alien with the rather nasty habit of inflicting, get this, sixth-degree burns on its victims. If Mulder's peek at the aliens in the sunken aircraft was accurate, a whole new set of aliens had decided to take an interest in poor Max! This time, instead of aliens themselves doing the incinerating quickly, Mulder and Scully ended up tracking the trail of radioactive spare parts that did the job at a much slower rate.

CASE CREDITS

WRITTEN BY: Chris Carter and
    Frank Spotnitz
DIRECTED BY: Kim Manners
ORIGINAL PRODUCTION
    NUMBER: 4X18
ORIGINAL US AIRDATE: 03/23/97

GUEST CAST

ASSISTANT DIRECTOR WALTER
S. SKINNER
    Mitch Pileggi
MAX FENIG
    Scott Bellis
AGENT PENDRELL
    Brendan Beiser
SCOTT GARRETT
    Greg Michaels
MR. BALLARD
    John Destry
SERGEANT ARMANDO GONZALES
    Rick Dobran
LAROLD REBHUN
    Jerry Schram
DARK MAN
    David Pálffy
PILOT
    Mark Wilson
CORPORAL FRISH
    Tom O'Brien
SHARON GRAFFIA
    Chilton Crane
BRUCE BEARFELD
    Robert Moloney
MOTEL MANAGER
    Felicia Shulman

DEATH TOLL

2 MEN: 1 shot to death,
    1 unaccounted for

introduced to Scully's father when he died and became part of a paranormal experience to rival anything Mulder might have investigated. Bill Mulder didn't last much longer. When Melissa Scully died, and there was no sign of either of her brothers during the entire drawn-out deathbed scene, fans began to wonder if the Scully boys hadn't figured something out and were making sure they weren't next. By the time X crawled along the floor to his death, jokes about the "red shirts" in *Star Trek* were beginning to circulate around office water-coolers.

So when the adorable Agent Pendrell arrived on the scene, with his puppy-dog eyes and his evident crush on Dana Scully, it was hard for fans to work up the enthusiasm his character might otherwise have enjoyed. Though many X-Philes delighted in Brendan Beiser's portrayal of the lovelorn agent, most felt his fate had already been written. If he didn't turn out to be the latest plant sent to derail the Dynamic Duo's investigations, then, obviously, he was being set up as the next body. What began as a wake-up call to fans made complacent by other programs, and what was certainly effective at the time, has become so commonplace that X-Philes are now more likely to be surprised when a character survives! Many were ready to write off the gut-shot Skinner without waiting for the end of act four. When Bill Mulder showed up at a family gathering, viewers were more interested in whether or not he'd make it to the credits alive than in yet another alien body. Even Mulder's apparent demise at the end of the fourth season drew no real fan uproar.

Having swung viewers through the spectrum of emotions, from shocked to blasé, how does a writer now convince those same viewers to invest energy and emotion in characters that may not be around next week? It's an interesting problem, one that W. C. Fields once described as "leaving them wanting less." Fields's solution to the problem, "Don't do it!" may be a bit late to benefit X-Philes.

CODE NAME:

"Synchrony"

Case: XF-4X19-04-13-97

CASE SUMMARY

Contradictory evidence strongly suggests that the man arrested for his friend's death, the man who is still sitting in jail, is also continuing to kill by a most unusual method – freezing his victims to death. Taking inspiration from Scully's graduate work, however, Mulder soon comes up with a theory that lets Jason Nichols be in two places at once – time travel.

CASE HISTORY
The Man: David William Duchovny

VITAL STATISTICS:
DOB: August 7, 1960
PLACE OF BIRTH: New York City
HEIGHT: 6'
HAIR: Brown
EYES: Hazel
IDENTIFYING MARK: Mole on right cheek
Parents: Amram and Margaret Ducovny [yes, that's the way he spells it]
SIBLINGS: Daniel (older), living in Los Angeles
Laurie (younger), living in New York City
MARITAL STATUS: Married to actress Tea Leoni, May 6, 1997
CHILDREN: None

EDUCATIONAL INFORMATION:
- Collegiate Prep, Manhattan
- Princeton University, BA
- Yale University, MA (English), Ph.D. (unfinished):
Dissertation: "Magic and Technology in Contemporary Poetry and Prose"
- The Actors Studio

RESIDENCES:
- Vancouver, British Columbia, Canada
- Malibu, California, USA

INTERESTS:
Sports, both individual (jogging, swimming, and yoga) and team (basketball and baseball).
Writing, including poetry. Music. Theater. Tea Leoni.

Filmography

X-Files:The Movie (1998) – Special Agent Fox Mulder

Playing God (1997) – Eugene Sands

"The Simpsons" [Springfield Files] (1997) – Voice of Special Agent Fox Mulder

"Duckman" [The Girls of Route Canal] (1996) – Voice of Richard

"Frasier" [Frasier Loves Roz] (1996) – Voice of Caller Tom

"Space: Above and Beyond" [R&R] (1996) – Handsome Alvin

"The Larry Sanders Show" [The Bump] (1995) – Himself

"Saturday Night Live" (1995) – Himself

"The X-Files" (1993–present) – Special Agent Fox Mulder

Kalifornia (1993) – Brian Kessler

"Red Shoe Diaries" (1992) – Jake

"Baby Snatcher" (1992) – David

Beethoven (1992) – Brad

Chaplin (1992) – Rollie Totherob

Ruby (1992) – Officer Tippit

Venice/Venice (1992) – Dylan

Denial (1991) – John

Don't Tell Mom the Babysitter's Dead (1991) – Bruce

Julia Has Two Lovers (1991) – Daniel

The Rapture (1991) – Randy

"Twin Peaks" (1990) – DEA Agent Dennis/Denise Bryson

Bad Influence (1990) – Club Goer

New Year's Day (1989) – Billy

Working Girl (1988) – Tess's Birthday Party Friend

The Character: Fox William Mulder

<u>PERSONNEL DOSSIER # 118-366-047</u>
NAME: Fox William Mulder
POSITION: Special Agent, Department of Justice, Federal Bureau of Investigation
CURRENTLY ASSIGNED: N/A
FBI BADGE ID#: JTTO 47101111
CONTACT#S: (Home) 202-555-0199

<u>PERSONAL INFORMATION:</u>
DOB: October 11, 1960 [It was later changed to October 13, 1960, in the episodes "Nisei" and "731."]
HEIGHT: 6'
HAIR: Medium Brown
EYES: Hazel
MARITAL STATUS: Single/Never Married/No Dependents
PARENTS: Father, William Mulder (deceased/murdered) Mother, (Elizabeth?) Mulder
SIBLINGS: One sister, Samantha T. Mulder, disappeared from the family home November 27, 1973. Whereabouts remain unknown.
IN CASE OF EMERGENCY: Agent Dana Scully, Washington Bureau
RELIGIOUS AFFILIATION: Not a matter of record.

<u>EDUCATIONAL INFORMATION:</u>
● Agent Mulder graduated Oxford with a degree in psychology.
● Graduated high in his FBI Training Academy (Quantico) class.

<u>WORK HISTORY (CHRONOLOGICAL):</u>
● Completed Psychology Residency

- Assigned Violent Crimes Section, Behavioral Sciences Unit
- Assigned X-Files, Field Agent
- Assigned Intelligence Division, Communications
- Reassigned X-Files, Field Agent

SUPERVISORY NOTES (CHRONOLOGICAL)

1. On the recommendation of his instructors, and in keeping with his graduate training, Agent Mulder has been assigned to the Behavioral Sciences Unit of the Violent Crimes Section.

2. An inquiry into the death of his former partner determined that Agent Mulder acted properly and was in no way responsible for the death of Agent Lamana.

3. A notation of exemplary service in the Props case has been added to this file.

4. At his own request, and with the consent of his superiors, Agent Mulder has undertaken the task of investigating some previously unsolved cases. It is anticipated that this is a temporary assignment to help clear a backlog, and that Agent Mulder will soon be returning to VCS.

5. As Agent Mulder shows no indication of returning to his previous assignment in the near future, an informal inquiry into the value of his present assignment will be instituted to determine if his skills might be better employed outside the X-Files.

6. Agent Dana Scully has been assigned to the X-Files and will be reporting directly to the administration.

7. Following some unorthodox investigations, it has been determined that Agent Mulder will be reassigned to a regular field position. (Transfer to Intelligence, Communications, and Surveillance).

8. Under the direction of Assistant Director Skinner, both agents Mulder and Scully have returned to their pursuit of the X-Files. Duration of this assignment has yet to be specified.

9. This agent's involvement in the unauthorized and irregular

---

THESE ARE THE EASY ONES! TAKE A SINGLE POINT FOR EACH CORRECT ANSWER.

1. What was Jason Nichols's field of study?

2. How did Dr. Yonechi die?

3. Where did Lucas Menand, Lisa Ianelli, and Jason Nichols work?

4. What went missing from M.I.T.'s computer?

5. How did Scully and the medical team save Lisa Ianelli?

THESE WILL MAKE YOU THINK, SO GIVE YOURSELF TWO POINTS FOR A CORRECT RESPONSE.

6. What time did the time traveller predict Lucas Menand would die?

7. At what seedy hotel did the time traveller stay?

8. What temperature was the body when Scully checked it first?

9. On what flight did Dr. Yonechi arrive?

10. Whose thesis did Mulder quote, twice, in this episode?

Trivia Buster

19

Answers

KEEP TRACK OF YOUR TOTAL SCORE. SEE WHERE YOU'D END UP IN THE X-FILEAN WORLD OF HIERARCHIES, SHADOW GOVERNMENTS, AND CONSPIRACIES.

ONE POINTERS:

1. Cryobiology.

2. He caught fire.

3. MIT, the Massachusetts Institute of Technology.

4. Jason Nichols's files.

5. They kept her in the temperature-controlled tub.

TWO POINTERS:

6. 11:46 p.m.

7. The Lighthouse.

8. 8⁰ Fahrenheit.

9. Pan Oceanic Flight #1701.

10. Scully's.

YOUR SCORE _____

activities of the Two Grey Hills Navajo reserve has been noted as further evidence of his inability to operate within the system. However, as his activities were unofficial, and could not be deemed illegal, no internal disciplinary action will be taken.

10. The Japanese Diplomatic Corps has filed formal requests for investigation into the actions of Agent Mulder in the wake of a string of deaths of Japanese personnel.

11. The requests on the part of the Japanese Diplomatic Corps have been dropped, no reason given.

12. Agent Mulder has formally declined to apply for a position in Special Agent Patterson's VCS unit.

13. Agent Mulder has formally declined to cooperate with writer Jose Chung. Request is being rerouted through Public Relations.

14. Despite some reservations by the OPC, Agent Mulder has accepted an invitation to appear at NICAP's AGM as the keynote speaker, his address loosely titled "The Case of Observer Credibility."

15. Charges laid against Agent Mulder for assaulting a superior agent, Assistant Director Walter Skinner, have been dropped at AD Skinner's express request.

16. Agent Mulder's request for permission to submit private photographs for analysis at the Washington Bureau labs has been denied.

17. Agent Mulder's travel expense forms, including two tickets to Russia, have been turned over to the Department of Justice's main accounting section for a determination of financial liability.

18. Follow-up to notation 17. As Special Agent Mulder's testimony before the Congressional committee was deemed to include information made possible by travel claimed in his expense vouchers, financial liability has been accepted by the Bureau.

19. Agent Mulder's request to follow up an earlier case has been approved, as has permission to share information with various agencies investigating the crash of Flight 549. All inter-agency courtesies to be extended.

20. This file closed due to the death of Special Agent Fox Mulder.

CASE NOTES
Back to the Future

When Stephen Hawking talks about time, it's not generally on a scale any of us poor schmoos who managed to eke out a passing grade in physics, only to forget it within days of graduation, could understand. He speaks of the birth of universes as casually as most people of their latest niece or nephew and of time as a semi-solid construct which might have dimensions – or even corners! Without a doubt, he sees the world a little differently than the rest of us. So when he reverses his own previous theories about "life, the universe, and everything," people sort of sit up and take notice – especially when what he's saying is that time travel just might, theoretically, be possible.

Not that the "impossibility" of time travel bothered writers. Science fiction has been playing with the edges of science – even anticipating it – for nearly a century. Of course, the best of science fiction veered towards the "science" and less towards the "fiction" for its plots. The biggest problem for those writing about time travel and science was deciding which model they'd incorporate into their fiction.

Einstein probably had no idea that his $E = mc^2$ would throw writers into such a tizzy, or that it would interfere with one of science fiction's favourite notions, namely faster-than-light (FTL) travel. Basically, the theory (along with its cousin the Theory of Special Relativity) says that things gain mass as they move closer to the speed of light. So, the faster something moves, the more mass it gains until, eventually, there comes a point at which there isn't enough energy to displace that much mass that fast. Therefore, FTL travel isn't possible.

And what does FTL travel have to do with time travel? Well, the mathematicians and physicists who like to play with impossibilities have crunched the numbers and determined that, relatively speaking, if you were travelling faster than light, time

would move at a different "speed" than it does at less than light speed. If you were to stop travelling, you would have moved through a different amount of time than the people you'd left behind. Therefore, you'd be in a different time, which, technically, is time travel.

When most of us think about time travel, however, we think in terms of a single time stream, with events as points along a time line, points we could visit at will. However, because of the mass/energy/speed problem, it seems that Einstein's relative universe precludes that whole notion. Then along came quantum physics, which portrayed the universe in slightly different terms. Instead of a single stream of events, quantum physics allows a multitude of possible results, possible time lines. For example, in one possibility, a person waits for the walk sign,

crosses safely, then keeps on walking home. There is, of course, an opposite possibility. The person anticipates the walk sign, doesn't quite make the far curb, is nailed by a pizza delivery van and never gets home. Two possibilities. Both are equally possible in the second before the person decides to wait or race the light. Quantum physics suggests that both possibilities continue to exist even after the decision is made. We only see the possibility in our time stream but, somewhere, in some other time line, the person does indeed die. The program "Sliders" is based on this premiss and, so far, there's little proof that there aren't millions of time lines running alongside our own. The trick, of course, is to get from one stream to the other! Fiction has found a dozen ways around that, naturally occurring and man-made, but science hasn't been that successful.

Luckily for those who want to keep some science in their science fiction, there is a way to overcome both the relativistic and the quantum limitations. Einstein's theory didn't just give us a nifty formula and some useful additions, it also predicted the fact that light will bend in the presence of gravity, that black holes act as they do and that space isn't flat – or smooth. Under specific circumstances, space can be bent, twisted and turned back on itself. Time, which is after all a function of space, can, therefore, also be bent, twisted and turned back on itself. What that effectively does is bring two points of time, two separate events, closer together. All that's required then is the energy to move from point to point and, by a rather ironic twist in Einstein's numbers, it doesn't have to be lot of energy – as long as it's only used for a short time!

Now, with time the issue, and not some impossible-to-obtain amount of energy, quantum physics can come back into play. The neat thing about the two models is that they aren't mutually exclusive and quantum physics deals in such small increments of time that, for all intents and purposes, two

CASE CREDITS

WRITTEN BY: Howard Gordon and
     David Greenwalt
DIRECTED BY: Jim Charleston
ORIGINAL PRODUCTION
     NUMBER: 4X19
ORIGINAL US AIRDATE: 04/13/97

GUEST CAST

JASON NICHOLS
     Joseph Fuqua
LISA IANELLI
     Michelle Fairman
LUCAS MENAND
     Jed Rees
DR. YONECHI
     Hiro Kanagawa
CHUCK LUKERMAN
     Jonathan Walker
DOCTOR
     Alison Matthews
CORONER
     Norman Armour
DESK CLERK
     Patricia Idlette
SECURITY COP
     Brent Chapman
UNIFORMED COP
     Terry Arrowsmith
DETECTIVE
     Aureleo Di Nunzio
BUS DRIVER
     Eric Buermeyer

DEATH TOLL

4/5 MEN: 1 fallen under bus,
     1 frozen to death, 1 burnt to death
     in hospital; 1, or 2, Jason Nichols

events can happen simultaneously and that's about as short a time interval as even Einstein's equations could demand.

So, when Steven Hawking starts talking about tachyons, particles that are suspected of travelling faster than the speed of light – backwards in time! – and wormholes and time loops, the foundation has already been laid and, at least theoretically, time travel can remain within the bounds of the good science that makes good science fiction.

CODE NAME:

"Small Potatoes"

Case: XF-4X20-04-20-97

EYEWITNESS STATEMENT

"On, uh, on behalf of all the women in the world, I seriously doubt this has anything to do with consensual sex. I think it involves some form of Rohypnol rape."

Special Agent Dana Scully

CASE SUMMARY

Five children are born in Martinsburg, West Virginia. They have the usual ten fingers and the usual ten toes. They also have something most *un*usual, a tail. As Mulder and Scully's investigations quickly reveal, they also have one more thing in common – their father! When all five women claim never to have laid eyes on Eddie Van Blundht, the father of their children, Scully's thinking Rohypnol while Mulder's wondering if Eddie isn't the latest in their list of shape-shifting mutants.

CASE HISTORY
The "Forget Pill" – Rohypnol

Any doctor worth a damn, if confronted with a pregnant woman who swore to have absolutely no memory of conception, would without doubt think Rohypnol instead of immaculate conception. To date, only one case of immaculate conception remains under serious scrutiny while at least six cases of Rohypnol rape, including two encounters that resulted in pregnancy, are currently before various American courts. One, given considerable air time just six to eight months before "Small Potatoes" was aired, brought the "date rape drug" onto the talk show discussion list and into common parlance in many American communities.

Rohypnol, a brand name for the group of drugs called flunitrazepam, is one of a new generation of drugs, highly engineered drugs, that's quickly becoming a darling among users and the "romantically challenged."

With its own litany of street names, everything from "roofies" to "roach," with "forget-me-yeahs," "R2," "rope," "la roche," and, of course, "rape," Rohypnol is *the* dream drug for any number of habitual users. Pop a single Rohypnol, at less than $5.00 US, with a single beer and enjoy that pleasantly poached feeling for as much as eight hours. Makes getting drunk almost affordable again! If cocaine is your drug of choice, Rohypnol takes care of the after-using crash. In fact, it so softens the landing that some people claim they just stay "a little above normal" for hours. But Rohypnol is a flexible drug, not only does it make the downs easier, it intensifies the highs. Some of the most sought after "combo packs" for users right now include heroin with the Rohypnol. It cranks up the high, smooths out the crash.

And it's *legal*!

Well, sort of, anyway. It's legally produced and sold in sixty countries and, at the time of writing, could be brought back into the United States (where most Rohypnol abuse seems concentrated), in any quantity, as long as the person bringing it back had a prescription. It's driving Drug Enforcement personnel crazy. Says one officer, "We watched hundreds of units come up from Tijuana in just one afternoon. The prescriptions these kids were carrying were *photocopies*! The doctor down there just had a bunch printed up to save the strain on his wrist – and he's perfectly within his rights to do so. There's nothing we can do to stop it coming in, just watch kids get into deeper trouble when it hits the street."

Drug abuse, while still a serious problem in literally thousands of American neighborhoods, is, unfortunately, slow news when the media is looking for a fresh headline. The "War on Drugs," having fulfilled its political purpose, has been very much on the back burner. And teens aren't listening either. They live with guns in school locker rooms, drive-by shootings, and the risk of AIDS every time they make out. Something that punches up a high or makes a beer go further just isn't going to frighten them off. It was Rohypnol and champagne that sent rock star Kurt Cobain into a coma state in Rome just before his eventual suicide. Everyone knows the coma was alcohol-involved, everyone knows he'd been in and out of rehab, everyone knows he died long before he might have, but, how many people realize it was Rohypnol that completely eradicated his drinking judgement?

No, what caught media attention was the "Forget Pill" and

Trivia Buster

20

THESE ARE THE EASY ONES! TAKE A SINGLE POINT FOR EACH CORRECT ANSWER.

1. Who did Amanda claim fathered her child?

2. Which letter of Edward H. Van Blundht's name was usually forgotten?

3. What "big plans" did Scully have for Friday night?

4. What did Mulder jokingly suggest he and Scully should shop for?

5. What did Eddie Van Blundht spell wrong – twice?

THESE WILL MAKE YOU THINK, SO GIVE YOURSELF TWO POINTS FOR A CORRECT RESPONSE.

6. How many times had Amanda seen *Star Wars*?

7. What alias does Mulder use for his phone sex account?

8. Who would Scully choose to be for a day?

9. What color cumberbund did Marcus, Scully's 12th grade love, wear to the prom?

10. What did "Baboo" call Eddie?

20

Answers

ONE POINTERS:

1. Luke Skywalker.

2. The silent "H" in Blundht.

3. Writing an article for the *Penology Review*. Take two points if you knew the title was "Diminished Acetylcholine Production in Recidivist Offenders."

4. China patterns.

5. Federal Bureau of Investigation.

TWO POINTERS:

6. 368.

7. Marty.

8. Eleanor Roosevelt.

9. Kelly green.

10. Sugar Patootie.

YOUR SCORE _____

"Date Rape Drug" titles that began to appear with increasing frequency as women – and girls – around the United States reported being raped while incapacitated by the drug.

At first, even some officials failed to recognize the danger inherent in Rohypnol. Some even claimed it was nothing more than "a way for a 'good girl' to have a good time and not catch hell from home." Nothing was further from the truth. The breakdown of inhibitions which drinkers noticed as they increased the amount of Rohypnol they took with alcohol was nothing compared to the complete and almost instant amnesia suffered by those taking even slightly higher dosages. Something else that abusers of the Rohypnol-alcohol combination quickly discovered? The drug is completely tasteless and completely odourless when mixed with alcohol. Two tablets, enough to render a fully-grown woman practically unconscious in less than ten minutes, dissolve in less than a second, less than the time it takes to look around for a friend, less than the time it takes to glance away and light a cigarette.

A frightening scenario was suddenly being acted out across the southern United States. Girl and female friend go to bar for a drink. Girl asks friend to watch her drink while she goes to powder her nose. Friend is distracted by one of a pair of young men asking if she dropped this compact/wallet/scarf/whatever. Other half of pair drops the tablets. Within half an hour, two sober, upright-appearing young men are "helping" their drunk dates home. Who would interfere? No one. And that's the complex version! Even simpler to spend some time smiling from the other end of the bar, order a drink for the lady, and, in the process of walking down the bar, drop the tablets and hand them over. Any glass left unattended for a single second was a potential danger, a trap that some victims might never realize had been sprung.

The drug, in those concentrations, has an entirely predictable course of effect. A slight sense of dizziness could be caused by anything, the drink itself, stooping to get a purse, or

The line that divides those in front of the camera from those behind it was blurred once again when Darin Morgan, famous for his scripts, came around to make his costume-less debut. But what a way to do it! Makes you wonder if he submitted the classic head-shot to casting . . . or maybe a completely different angle?

even skipping lunch, in short, nothing frightening. The growing disorientation is too similar to drunkenness to arouse anyone's attention. The simultaneous chills and sweats the victims suffers next are psychological, not physical. No one watching the process would realize the distinct mental displacement behind something as innocent as a shiver. And nausea? How many people have been to a bar regularly and *not* seen someone get sick? That nausea is usually the attacker's cue to get in there, quickly. Less than fifteen minutes after ingesting the drug, as little as two minutes after beginning to feel a little queasy, the victim may no longer be able to call for help. Enunciation is severely impaired in Rohypnol poisoning and is swiftly followed by difficulty moving and, finally, unconsciousness.

The amnesia experienced by victims is as real as that suffered by any patient under a general anaesthesia. Ask Aunt Matilda how much she remembers about her appendectomy and you've some notion of just how little these victims recall. It's the amnesia that creates real difficulties, not only for the unfortunate victim, but for the law enforcement personnel trying to prosecute the case! In any criminal proceeding, the victim must give some evidence of a crime having occurred. In most cases, eye witness testimony is considered a baseline necessity. Victims of Rohypnol may have no direct memory or proof that they were raped. Unconscious victims seldom fight back so there are normally no defensive injuries. Unconscious victims also typically lack the vaginal bruising and tearing normally associated with a rape. Unless the victim realizes what may have happened during her "blackout," and immediately seeks the assistance of someone with a rape kit available, the embarrassed woman is just as likely to shower away whatever evidence would have supported her claim.

As more cases hit both the courts and the news, however, some changes are being made. Use of Rohypnol in a date-rape situation is now a felony under American law and, with felonies carrying sentences of up to twenty years, not to mention fines of a quarter of a million dollars, it's possible some few frat boys will have second thoughts. The real answer, of course, as always, is education, but that might come slowly. Rohypnol is currently still on the "easy-import" section of the Customs list. Testing for Rohypnol remains expensive, and few law enforcement jurisdictions outside of Florida and Texas seem inclined to test for its use – even in situations where alcohol levels alone can't account for dangerous driving. While several flyers have been sent out across the country, supposedly alerting police to the possibility of Rohypnol in their area, a survey by the College Womens' Association revealed that less than 8 percent of officers participating in the survey realized the "date-rape drug" was Rohypnol! If supposedly on-the-ball officials in law enforcement and customs stations haven't grasped the problem, how can the information trickle down to women who just want a drink after work?

Clarrise S., who is taking a former acquaintance back to court following his conviction on Rohypnol-involved rape, has a little more at stake than even the other victims whose cases are pending. In May of 1997, nine months after her rape, Ms. S. delivered an eight-pound baby boy in desperate and immediate need of specialized medical care – and organ transfer tissue. "I had no idea who'd done this to me, I knew before Joshua was born that there weren't any possible donors in my family, and, without a dedicated police investigation and some sympathetic prosecutors, I'd have no idea where to look next. Luckily, his paternal uncle appears to be a match and we can hope, but, even two years ago, my case, the case that proved who Joshua's father was, would have been thrown out for 'lack of evidence.'"

CASE NOTES
Guest Filmography: Christine Cavanaugh

Though a delightful actress, Christine Cavanaugh is one of those performers who inspire audiences to "I know the voice, I just can't place the face . . . ?" In Christine's case, however, that might well be a compliment. In addition to her wonderful live performances, she's lent her vocal talents to some marvellous, and unforgettable, roles.

Delivery (1997) – Bridgette

Babe (1995) – The Voice of Babe

Balto (1995)

"Night Stand" [One Night Stand Reunions] (1995) – Kathy

Little Surprises (1995) – Pepper

"Argh!!! Real Monsters" (1994) – Oblina

The Critic (1994) – The Voice of Marty Sherman

Mixed Nuts (1994) – The Voice of the Police

"Sonic the Hedgehog" (1993) – The Voice of Bunnie Rabbot

"Darkwing Duck" (1991) – The Voice of Gosalyn Mallard

"Herman's Head" (1992) – Martha

"Rugrats" (1991) – The Voice of Chuckie Finster

"Empty Nest" (1988) – Kimberly

The Tale of the Tail

Scully's assessment of the "tails" found on the Martinsburg babies was right on the money. Caudal appendages, as these "tails" are more often called in medical circles do, occasionally, turn up, as do other body parts that, though present at birth, are reassimilated back into the body. Some children are born with extra nipples, some with considerable amounts of webbing between their fingers or toes, none of which stays with

X HMMM? The fall from the attic didn't hurt Eddie Sr.'s tail, but Mulder's gentle touch cracked it off completely?

X CATCH IT? When Eddie, in Mulder form, is making himself at home in Mulder's office, one of the photos over his shoulder, on the bulletin board, is of Flukeman, Darin's other XF role.

X CATCH IT? Some fans wore out their tapes gathering all the information printed on Mulder's driver's license. Save your tape! His license number is 123-32-132, issued in the Commonwealth of Virginia. It was issued on 12-13-94, and expires 03-31-99. His date of birth is 10-13-61. Sex: M Height: 6-0 MULDER, FOX 42-2630 NEGAL PLACE ALEXANDRIA, VA 23242 And, despite his supposed red-green color blindness, there's no apparent restrictions on his license.

CASE CREDITS

WRITTEN BY: Vince Gilligan
DIRECTED BY: Clifford Bole
ORIGINAL PRODUCTION
    NUMBER: 4X20
ORIGINAL US AIRDATE: 04/20/97

GUEST CAST

ASSISTANT DIRECTOR WALTER
S. SKINNER
    Mitch Pileggi
EDDIE VAN BLUNDHT
    Darin Morgan
AMANDA NELLIGAN
    Christine Cavanaugh
DR. ALTON PUGH
    Robert Rozen
HEALTH DEPARTMENT DOCTOR
    P. Lynn Johnson
DEPUTY
    David Cameron
ANGRY HUSBAND
    Paul McGillion
ANGRY WIFE
    Jennifer Sterling
SECOND HUSBAND
    Peter Kelamis
O.R. NURSE
    Constance Barns
DUTY NURSE
    Carrie Cain Sparks
SECOND NURSE
    Monica Gemmer
SECURITY GUARD
    Forbes Angus

them for life and little of which is usually apparent even three months later.

To call these organs "vestigial," however, isn't quite right. Vestigial implies that these "organs" were once useful and have simply de-evolved in some way. The Creationist – Evolutionist Argument makes much of these organs, both pro and con, but often fails to rely on even basic science to support their position. Take the so-called "vestigial" appendix. For some time, the argument was that the appendix was a wasted away organ that had once fulfilled the same purpose as the cecum, an organ in many mammals where specialized bacteria break down cellulose. That theory makes little sense when reviewed with the certain knowledge that a significant proportion of mammals have *both* a cecum and an appendix. Obviously, one isn't a vestigial form of the other. The appendix, like tonsils and adenoids, which were also once called vestigial, is part of the lymphatic system.

Likewise, male mammary glands, breasts, can't be considered "vestigial" if they were *never* used to nurse young, not at any time in human evolution. While many well-educated people will agree the male of the species never breast-fed anything, they continue to think of appendixes and "tails" as "vestigial."

So, what are tails? They aren't signs of evolution – or devolution for that matter.

They are usually, as was the case when the last "human tail" was reported in the prestigious *The New England Journal of Medicine*, a fatty mass as unlike a real tail as it's possible to be. They have no bones or cartilage to support musculature. Then again, they have no musculature so the bones would be sort of redundant, and, without musculature, there'd be no nifty "wiggling effect" for the crew from Area 51's computer graphics division to add in to the opening sequence.

And what is the purpose of this fatty mass?

Well, no one quite seems to know – but that doesn't make it *vestigial*!

CODE NAME:

"Zero Sum"

Case: XF-4X21-04-27-97

Who'd have thought we'd
see Skinner in skivvies?

CASE SUMMARY

Assistant Director Walter S. Skinner, in a bid to find a cure for a desperately ill Agent Scully, has made a pact with the Devil, a pact he'd already advised Mulder against! Fulfilling the terms of his "deal" with The Cigarette-Smoking Man becomes impossible, however, when Skinner discovers the rules were changed without his knowledge and he finds himself deep in an apparent conspiracy to test biological agents on American soil. Under circumstances he could never have predicted, Skinner learns first-hand just how tenacious an investigator Special Agent Fox Mulder can be.

CASE HISTORY
"... Even Bees Do It"

"Any kind of bee can be lethal provided you get stung by enough of them. Even Africanized honey bees and so-called killer bees basically have the same venom as the European honey bee. It's just that they tend to attack in swarms." – THE BEE GUY

As dozens of Americans have discovered since African honey bees escaped from their new home in Brazil over four decades ago, Skinner's outside expert knew what he was talking about. The other major difference between the European bees and their Africanized cousins is the time it takes to get them really ticked off. While European bees will tolerate a considerable amount of intrusion into their harvesting areas, and even allow humans to pass by their nests if the humans don't actually physically disturb them, Africanized hives strenuously enforce their own version of a "zero tolerance" policy. It's not a matter of temperament, as is often suggested in films like the infamous *Swarm*, where bees seemed intent on hunting down particular victims, but a matter of biology.

In the bee world, there are basically two sorts of survival tactics. One encourages bees to be diligent little workers who happily gather resources that will allow the hive to survive over long, cold winters. The other survival plan, practised by most tropical bees, which of course includes the African honey bee

which evolved in the warmth of the savannah of south-east Africa, doesn't include cold winter storage because there are no cold winters in the tropics. It does, however, include an aggressive reproductive schedule. While the European bees hunker down and try to survive over the winter, the tropical bees just keep replacing those that die, an intensive sort of activity with rigorous demands on the hives, and most of their behavioral differences stem from this aggressive strategy. Though African honey bees were first brought to the Americas because of the huge amounts of honey they produce year-round, while other bees settle in to survive and eat their reserves, little African bee honey is stored at all, because it's constantly being used by the exploding population of the nest. In Africa, where food resources are more consistently available than in North America (where the flowers that produce nectar virtually disappear for months at a stretch), swarms rise on a fairly regular basis to distribute the nest population over a wider area. In North America, however, swarms frequently rise for the sole purpose of "absconding," deserting their nest entirely to take over one or more European nests which are already rich in stored food. During these irregular swarming periods, the Africanized bees are homeless and unsettled, and may be travelling with a single adult queen which they will protect at any cost.

Even after the bees have taken over a previously occupied nest, or settled into a new one of their own making, the logistics of their population make them more dangerous than other bees. For starters, Africanized hives contain up to five times as many guards as European bees. The hiker who accidentally steps close enough to shake the hive is, therefore, immediately at five times the risk of being stung. A PGA golfer and his caddie, participating in an event in Arizona, were stung twenty and eighty times respectively, which immediately made headlines. Had the golfer approached a European hive, and been stung by a proportionate number of bees, in this case four, no one would likely have even heard of the incident.

21

THESE ARE THE EASY ONES! TAKE A SINGLE POINT FOR EACH CORRECT ANSWER.

1. Name the first victim.

2. Which item of evidence did Skinner switch?

3. Boxers or briefs? Which does Skinner prefer?

4. How many boxes did Marita claim were sent from Canada?

5. Who turned up in the bank surveillance photos?

THESE WILL MAKE YOU THINK, SO GIVE YOURSELF TWO POINTS FOR A CORRECT RESPONSE.

6. Who e-mailed the crime scene photos to Mulder?

7. Name the school where the bees attacked.

8. How many shots did Skinner fire in this episode?

9. What fate did the entomologist meet?

10. What did Skinner find dripping down the bathroom wall?

Trivia Buster

21

Answers

KEEP TRACK OF YOUR TOTAL SCORE. SEE WHERE YOU'D END UP IN THE X-FILEAN WORLD OF HIERARCHIES, SHADOW GOVERNMENTS, AND CONSPIRACIES.

ONE POINTERS:

1. Jane L. Brody.

2. A blood sample.

3. Briefs.

4. 7.

5. Assistant Director Walter S. Skinner.

TWO POINTERS:

6. Det. Ray Thomas.

7. JFK Elementary School.

8. 3.

9. He was stung to death.

10. Honey.

YOUR SCORE: _____

The caddie, stung by a proportionate number of sixteen, would likely have gotten local mention in the news, but it would hardly have been the talk of the season, or even of the week.

It's not just sheer numbers that make Africanized bees dangerous; they also range far beyond the area covered by European bees. Though some European bees are seldom seen more than 500 feet from their hives, Africanized bees can range up to a mile from their nest. They also forage for longer periods of time, frequently beginning before sunrise and working late into the night to supply the constant demand for food within the nest. Both these gathering strategies increase the likelihood of encounters between humans and Africanized bees in the first place.

And there are circumstances that make even the calmest of "killer bees" more likely to swarm or to attack. Conditions within the hive, the heat, the humidity, the number of individuals, the number of queens, the quantity and quality of nectar available, and even the proximity of European honey bee hives. Africanized bees don't take over other hives merely by swarming attacks, they also rise to meet mating European queen bees, with which they can easily interbreed. The flight paths of queen bees are determined by factors common to both species and it's not uncommon for clouds of Africanized bees to anticipate flights, arriving to mate long before males from the queen's own group. As queens mate just once in a lifetime, all offspring born into the nest will carry the dominant Africanized traits. Heat and humidity also seem to play roles in swarming behaviour. In addition to keeping agitated bees aroused for hours longer than usual, hot and humid air carries pheromones much better than cold air can, because it is also usually lacking in moisture. Like social ants, some bees are suspected of releasing alarm odours when they sting or just before death. Within a population that's easily roused, such pheromones can induce the equivalent of a shark feeding frenzy.

In reviewing "Zero Sum," however, it's difficult to determine what, if anything, set off the even more touchy *X-File*an bees . . . The bees who'd set up housekeeping in the Postal Routing Center bathroom attacked a woman was doing nothing except sitting and smoking. The previous occupant, who washed her hands in a sink directly next to the hive, wasn't swarmed, yet, despite a haze of smoke, which usually makes bees less aggressive, Jane Brody was swarmed, attacked, and killed! Even more surprising, however, is the death of the entomologist. From a section of comb that would easily fit in a mayonnaise jar, a virtual horde of bees emerged! While the more suspicious fan might surmise that the population had been significantly, not to mention deliberately, increased by whoever left the incubator door open, it's still difficult to understand why the bees would decide to cluster around light bulbs and windows rather than seek the corners and crevices where they might conceivably be able to start a hive. The Hitchcock-styled attack in the schoolyard, eerily reminiscent of *The Birds*, is both the most typical and the most unlikely attack of all! While playgrounds have indeed been the scenes of attacks previously, it would be highly unusual for a colony of Africanized bees to establish themselves anywhere in the vicinity of the sort of noise most playgrounds produce pretty regularly. Of course, all X-Philes know that was a set-up to test the bees' ability to carry disease, so it's doubtful there ever was a hive . . .

And just how remote is the idea of smallpox-carrying bees? In theory, probably not remote at all. Just as the malaria carried by mosquitoes and the plague carried by fleas can easily be passed on to humans, it's possible, even if only at the extreme edge of possibility, that bees could carry some strain of some disease to which people could succumb. Just as the "killer bees" play off a popular modern paranoia, the threat of new diseases as vigorous and aggressive as, for example, ebola or AIDS, is another "just possible" fear that can be stirred in to the mixture of conspiracy and myth for which *The X-Files* is justifiably renowned.

X HMMMM? How did all those bees get past the water trap of the sink? Most insects, bees included, are blessed/cursed with an open respiratory system. They can't exactly hold their breath!

X If nothing else, Marita is a persistent caller. She let the phone ring right through the torturous scene between Skinner and The Cigarette-Smoking Man so that CSM could pick it up some ten rings later!

Mitch Pileggi modelled
Skinner after his own father.

MITCH PILEGGI

D.O.B.: April 5, 1952
HEIGHT: 6' 2"
HOMETOWN: Currently, Valencia, California
BORN: Portland, Oregon
PARENTS: Maxine and Vito Pileggi
SIBLINGS: five brothers and sisters
FACTS:

● Graduated with a degree in business from the University of Texas, Austin.

● Divorced from Debbie Andrews in 1983, shortly after he moved to Los Angeles to pursue an acting career, he married Arlene Rempel, Gillian Anderson's stand-in, in Hawaii last year.

● Lived in Turkey, Germany, and Saudi Arabia. He was in Iraq during the coup and was happy enough to return to the United States and look for a new line of work.

NOTEBOOK

Behind the Desk

Sitting behind a desk with a prominent NO SMOKING sign is Mitch Pileggi. He'll run through take after take with the professionalism one might expect of his *X-File* an alter ego, Walter Sergei Skinner, but that's where the similarity seems to end.

With the take in the can, he might kick back and light up one of the cigarettes Skinner abhors, and, before long, will be guaranteed to have half the cast and crew in stitches from the sort of genuine laughter and enthusiasm that often makes it difficult for people to place him as the rather dour Assistant Director away from the set. Then again, it's hard to imagine Skinner on rollerblades, a not uncommon sight for those living near the actor himself!

- Auditioned for other *X-Files* roles but was passed over for having a shaved head. After auditioning the part of Skinner, with hair, he not only appeared in "Tooms," but several second-season episodes, then got the green light for better billing and a six-year contract! Oddly enough, that smooth pate is one of the items most frequently cited by fans as his most sexy feature!
- Had never seen an episode until after his first appearance in "Tooms."
- Cites his "out-of-body" experience dialog as his personal favorite scene.
- Prior to the episode "Avatar," Pileggi didn't think it likely that Skinner would be married. At the end of season four, with the on-again-off-again showing of that wedding band, X-Philes are still wondering!
- Unlike his colleagues David Duchovny, who has racked up some story credits already, and Gillian Anderson, who says she "might" be interested in some behind the camera experience, Mitch Pileggi has no desire to do anything other than act – luckily for those fans who enjoy even his briefest appearances.
- With his character's jaw having been a target for Mulder, Krycek, Krycek's buddy Louis Cardinal, X, and even little Holly, the clerk from "Pusher," Pileggi qualifies as the "actor most likely to end up getting punched in an episode of *The X-Files*."

Filmography

Raven Hawk (1996) – Carl Rikker
Vampire in Brooklyn (1995) – Tony
Dangerous Touch (1994) – Vince
*"Pointman" (*1994) – Benny
"Trouble Shooters: Trapped Beneath the Earth" (1993) – Thompson
Basic Instinct (1992) – Internal Affairs Investigator
Guilty as Charged (1991) – Dominque

X CATCH IT? The bees for this episode were created by Digital Universe, CBS Animation.

X This episode was dedicated to the memory of Vito J. Pileggi, Mitch Pileggi's father and his inspiration for the highly principled and intense Assistant Director Walter S. Skinner.

X HMMMM? So, the Federal Bureau of Investigation couldn't come up with a serial number? Considering the fact that they've been doing it for years with an acid test that's so far proved remarkably reliable, X-Philes will have to wonder just what The Cigarette-Smoking Man – or perhaps even Mulder himself! – really did to that gun.

WRITTEN BY: Howard Gordon and
   Frank Spotnitz
DIRECTED BY:Kim Manners
ORIGINAL PRODUCTION
   NUMBER: 4X21
ORIGINAL US AIR DATE: 04/27/97

GUEST CAST

ASSISTANT DIRECTOR WALTER
S. SKINNER
   Mitch Pileggi
CIGARETTE-SMOKING MAN
   William B. Davis
MARITA COVARRUBIAS
   Laurie Holden
GRAY-HAIRED MAN
   Morris Panych
FIRST ELDER
   Don S. Williams
SECOND ELDER
   John Moore
PHOTO TECHNICIAN
   Christopher J. Newton
AGENT KAUTZ
   Paul McLean
DET. HUGEL
   Fred Keating
DET. THOMAS
   Uncredited
DR. PETER VALEDESPINO
   Allan Gray
DR. EMILE LINZER
   Barry Creene
LISA STEWART
   Jane Brody
MISTY
   Nicolle Nattrass
MRS. KEMPER
   Theresa Puskar
BESPECTACLED BOY
   Addison Ridge

DEATH TOLL

UNKNOWN NUMBER OF CHILDREN:
   all by bee stings/smallpox
2 MEN: 1 shot to the head,
   1 bee sting/smallpox
2 WOMEN: bee sting/smallpox

"Knight Rider" (1990) – Thomas J. Watts
"Doctor Doctor" [Ice Follies] (1990) – Coach
"Night Visions" (1990) – Keller
Brothers in Arms (1989) – Caleb
Shocker (1989) – Horace Pinker
"China Beach" [With a Little Help From My Friends] (1989)
"Alien Nation" [The Night of the Screams] (1989) – John Paul Sartre
Return of the Living Dead Part II (1988) – Sarge
Death Wish 4: The Crackdown (1987) – Cannery Lab Foreman
Three O'Clock High (1987) – Duke Herman
"Hooperman" [Baby Talk] (1987)
"Three on a Match" (1987) – Bull
Rio Abajo (1984) – Stephens
"The Sky's No Limit" (1984) – John
Mongrel (1982) – Woody

Appearances on *The X-Files*

Hard as it is to believe, the Skinner character didn't become a player on *The X-Files* until its second season. If it seems like longer, it's likely because his screen time has been increasing on a fairly consistent basis since the beginning and so many of his appearances are tied to the "mythology" episodes, those shows that deal directly with the search for Mulder's Proof and the role of government conspiracies and cover-ups.

Appearances on *The X-Files:*

Season One: 1 episode	Season Three: 9 episodes	Season Four: 13 episodes	
"Tooms"	*"End Game"*	*"Avatar"*	*"Terma"*
	"F. Emasculata"	*"Wetwired"*	*"El Mundo Gira"*
	"Anasazi"	*"Talitha Cumi"*	*"Memento Mori"*
			"Unrequited"
Season Two: 9 episodes	*"The Blessing Way"*	*"Herrenvolk"*	*"Tempus Fugit"*
"Little Green Men"	*"Paper Clip"*	*"Teliko"*	*"Max"*
"The Host"	*"Grotesque"*	*"The Field Where I Died"*	*"Small Potatoes"*
"Sleepless"	*"Piper Maru"*	*"Paper Hearts"*	*"Zero Sum"*
"Ascension"	*"Apocrypha"*	*"Tunguska"*	
"One Breath"	*"Pusher"*		*32 episodes total*
"Colony"			

CODE NAME:

"Elegy"

Case: XF-4X22-05-04-97

CASE SUMMARY

A series of young women are violently murdered and police quickly suspect that Harold Spuller, a man who voluntarily signed himself into a mental hospital, is the killer. Mulder, however, suspects that the young man's involvement, though equally intimate, is on another level altogether. When Spuller foresees the unexpected death of his boss, a death he could have had no part in, the finger of suspicion must move on.

CASE HISTORY
Apparitions of Death

This episode of The *X-Files* took an old legend and, in giving it a new twist, also managed to weave in a little of its own mythology. The spectre of Death, whether as the European's caped figure carrying farm equipment or the slightly more welcoming tree spirits of the Nagawitha, is common to almost every human mythos. The Vikings had their Valkyries, the Tartar tribes had Vighis, a skeletal woman riding across the plains to take the fallen heroes on to the next existence. Though most of these supernatural beings appeared only to those about to die, some few also appeared to others. As Mulder notes, the Irish had the fetch which Brand's *Popular Antiquities* defines as spirits "most likely to appear to distant friends and relations at the very instant preceding the death of those they represented." John Shiban took some of that lore, then kinked just a tad to the left, making his disembodied spirits visible not to the friends and relatives of the deceased, but to another person close to death, in this case Harold Spuller and Scully herself. Small wonder that was a club Scully wanted no membership in.

Ghost stories are probably the most persistent of human folk tales. Whether it's because, like roller-coaster fanatics, we just love to be scared, or because we want to believe there's something besides an opportunity to fertilize our patch of ground after death, humanity in general is enamoured of ghost stories.

Ireland, home not only to the fetch but also the bansidhe and hosts of other supernaturals including a "bottle imp" that sounds remarkably like Aladdin's genie, is full of stories that tie the living, the dead, the almost dead, and the very dead together.

A tale out of western Ireland could have been a template for "Elegy." The Garrow-Ghast, a fetch of a slightly different stripe, took it upon herself to warn the Darrow family whenever anyone in the area was about to die an unjust death. Why the Darrow family remains somewhat obscure, though, if Irish traditions holds true, it would likely turn out that the Darrows themselves had done something "unjust" at one point and the regular visitations of the Garrow-Ghast were a form of punishment, or appeasement, in themselves. In any case, if it was the Garrow-Ghast's self-appointed task to warn the Darrows of impending disaster to one of their neighbors, the Darrows' task was to do something about it! Not doing something about it wasn't an option. If they managed to intervene in time to prevent the death, the Garrow-Ghast just screamed about the house for a single night, the warning night. If they ignored her and the neighbor died, she screamed the house down night after night until the next new moon.

The first man "rescued" by the Garrow-Ghast, an Albert Dunney, was, after a profitable day in the market square, taking himself and his earnings home when he was set upon by robbers. Though his pockets were plenty heavy for the times, the robbers figured that where there was that much good coin, there was probably more at home. So, instead of robbing him, coshing him on the head and leaving him there, they lugged him off to their hiding spot and sent a note to his family asking for a ransom. Unfortunately for Albert Dunney, there was no more money at home, a fact he was all too well aware of! He might still have been dumped along a convenient road when the truth came out if not for a piece of bad luck. The

22

THESE ARE THE EASY ONES! TAKE A SINGLE POINT FOR EACH CORRECT ANSWER.

1. What was written in the wax of the bowling lane?

2. Who did the patients at the mental hospital i.d. as the killer?

3. What did the strings of numbers Harold quoted refer to?

4. What was Mr. Pintero's cause of death?

5. Who was Harold Spuller's roommate at the hospital?

THESE WILL MAKE YOU THINK, SO GIVE YOURSELF TWO POINTS FOR A CORRECT RESPONSE.

6. Name the lanes where Harold Spuller worked.

7. What was served at the New Horizon Psychiatric Center the night of the 911 call?

8. Which lane was broken?

9. What was Michelle Chamberlain's shoe size?

10. Name any two of the victims.

22

Answers

ONE POINTERS:

1. SHE IS ME.

2. Jay Leno.

3. Bowling scores.

4. Heart attack.

5. Chuck Forsch.

TWO POINTERS:

6. Angie's Midnight Bowl.

7. Sloppy Joes.

8. 6.

9. 6 and a half.

10. Penny Timmons, Risa Shapiro, Michelle Chamberlain, Lauren Heller. *Take three points if you remembered more than two.*

YOUR SCORE _____

bag covering his head, not to mention half smothering him, had been loosened by the crew as the day wore on. When they attempted to shove him back in his hidey-hole that night, it fell off, revealing the faces of his kidnappers. Now, money or no money, he wasn't getting loose. He knew it. The gang knew it. All that was left was to determine *how* and *where* to dispose of him. For that, the crew decided to get everyone together, something that would have looked even more suspicious at night. Instead, they'd meet in the morning.

That night, the Garrow-Ghast made her first visit to the Darrow farm. The screaming and the sound of rocks skittering across the roof of the cottage soon had everyone either out of their beds or under them. Gerald Darrow, the oldest man present, took two of his sons and some solid rake handles out around the house, but found nothing. Inside, however, his youngest boy, Harold, was pointing at the ghostly image of Albert Dunney! The spirit hung upright in the center of the main room, twirling about slowly as if hung. Naturally, Harold and the rest of the family passed the message on to the others outside who, while still inundated by the sounds of the screaming, couldn't find its source. Scared half witless, Harold and his brothers set off to the Dunney farm to see if anything was wrong. They met his wife and two of his children on the road, all searching for Albert Dunney. With the Dunneys' knowledge of the route Albert usually took, some shrewd ideas about who in the area might be up to such tricks, and the Darrows' contribution to the search, a set of three good oil lanterns which quickly helped pick up the spot where the struggle took place, and the direction Albert Dunney was dragged off in, it didn't take long to find the shack, the two left to guard it, and Albert Dunney tied up under a cot-bed. A good brawl soon had the Dunneys and Darrows on their way home with the two watchers dragged along for delivery to the local courts in the morning. The only piece of misfortune was that young Harold, who'd first seen the vision of Dunney twisting in the imaginary wind, caught an off-balance swing by one of Dunney's abductors. In something of a freak accident, he fell over backwards, smacked his usually hard head against the corner of a chair or table and died!

Still, accidents happen and farming families always seemed to be at risk for one injury or another. The Dunneys went home, the Darrows mourned their dead son, and everything went back to normal.

Until the next time.

Nearly two years later, the same horrid screaming, and the same sound of something skittering across the roof, roused the Darrow household. Again, nothing could be seen outside, but the screaming didn't quiet at all until one of the Darrow boys, whose name is lost to time, pointed up towards the lower eave of the cottage. The silvery apparition of Clarice Findle, a near neighbor of the Darrows, appeared to slip and fall to the ground. Not surprisingly, the Darrows hurried off to the neighboring farm to inquire after Clarice's health. Her startled parents hurried to her room, only to discover she wasn't in bed at all. While they might not have been attentive, they weren't stupid and quickly guessed that young Clarice had probably snuck out to spend time with the young man she'd been 'sweet on' for several months. Now, where would they be? The nameless Darrow boy, recalling the image of the falling woman, suggested they hurry along the cliffs between the Findle farm and the farm of her young beau.

Even before they could properly see anyone on the cliffs ahead, both families knew they were on the right path when they heard the solid, real-world screams of a young woman. Rounding the edge of the cliff path, they found Clarice and her beau in a heated argument, Clarice's feet dangerously near the edge of the path and her beau pushing her hard in the direction of the water. Darrow's unremembered son raced

ahead, dragged the girl back onto the path, exchanged some heated comments with her suitor and, before any of the rest of the family could intervene, had gotten into an hand-to-hand fight with a man who had him on weight, height and reach. The unsung hero of this incident may have gotten in a swing or two of his own, but, if so, history doesn't record it. What is remembered is that the young Darrow boy, in rescuing Clarice Findle from a suitor who didn't want her, or the baby she'd just told him was coming, fell from the path and died two days later.

It's hardly surprising, considering the way the household was being weeded away, that the Darrows tried ignoring the Garrow-Ghast's next house call. Instead of haring off to see what might be wrong at the town's smithshop, home of the next vision the Garrow-Ghast brought, the Darrows lit some lamps, covered their ears and refused to budge from the house. The screaming continued all night, nearly driving Mrs. Darrow mad anyway. The sounds of rocks and feet on the roof grew even more violent. At one point, a wind blew down the chimney so hard it put out the fire in the grate! Still the family stayed put. It was the Darrows' youngest child, Karin, who'd been first to see the visions this time and, regardless of the howling surrounding the house, a noise none of the visiting tradesmen or other neighbors seemed to hear when they came by, neither of her parents would allow the child out of the house. When news came that the blacksmith's apprentice was dead, and the blacksmith blamed for his death after smacking the boy an angry, thoughtless blow with his hammer, the Darrows hoped for some relief. They got none until the moon changed its face once more. For thirty-four

NOTEBOOK

Guest Filmography: Alex Bruhanski

The X-Files excels at casting great character actors in even the smallest parts and Alex Bruhanski is certainly among the best.

A Daughter's Secret: The Traci di Carlo Story (1994) – Roger Horn

"Sin & Redemption" (1994) – Mr. Farley

"Dead Ahead: The Exxon Valdez Disaster" (1992) – Chuck O'Donnell

The Hitman (1991) – Scarlini

"Neon Rider" (1990) – C.C.

Bird on a Wire (1990) – Raun

Look Who's Talking Too (1990) – Needle Doctor

Cousins (1989) – Herbie

The Experts (1989) – Taxi Driver

Look Who's Talking (1989) – Street Worker

The Penthouse (1989) – Captain Mundy

"Higher Ground" (1988) – Donoso

"The Red Spider" (1988) – Sissy Mayo

"After the Promise" (1987) – Hospital Cop

"Hands of a Stranger" (1987) – Bluestone

"MacGyver" [Back From the Dead] (1987) – Sal

days, they lived like vampires, grabbing what sleep they could during the day and knowing they'd get none at night.

Needless to say, things didn't go well for the Darrows that growing season. A dull, damp season had already made an overabundant harvest an impossibility, but, with their household in chaos and their few workers having already run off, the Darrows barely brought in enough to keep them through the winter. Karin died in February after two weeks of fever and coughing, but of no specific disease that anyone could identify.

Even spring brought little relief when, just as planting season was due, and the Darrows had managed to lure back a few hands to help, they were once again awakened by the yowling sound of the Garrow-Ghast. The family's patriarch ordered his family to stay in their beds, to pull the sheets and the pillows up over their heads, to squeeze their eyes together and keep them shut. And it just might have worked. The violent winds that seemed to accompany the Garrow-Ghast's appearance grew stronger the longer she was ignored, and, just before dawn, the inner shutter on one of the windows flew open. Mr. Darrow's eyes opened, just for a fraction of a second, just long enough to see his sister's face screaming silently in through the wind at him. Ordering his family to stay where they were, and taking no one with him, he raced across the fields to the adjoining allotment where he found her cottage in flames. Two of her older children stood outside. Their mother and father, still inside, were handing down the three youngest ones through a small door in the upper loft area. The remainder of the tale remains a bit muddled, but, it seems he went inside after part of the ceiling began to fall, held the last child while his brother-in-law jumped to the ground, then helped both his sister and his nephew through before being caught under the rest of the roof.

The Garrow-Ghast never returned to Darrow Farm, but,

even if she had, she'd have found no Darrows there. Within hours of learning of her husband's death, Mrs. Darrow and her remaining children and grandchildren had packed their bags and disappeared.

While the tale of the Garrow-Ghast follows all the usual strictures for its genre, this particular story, like Shiban's, works best because of its eccentric qualities. In Ireland, no one questions the fact that it was the Darrows who were cursed. No one

CASE CREDITS

WRITTEN BY: John Shiban
DIRECTED BY: Jim Charleston
ORIGINAL PRODUCTION
    NUMBER: 4X22
ORIGINAL US AIRDATE: 05/04/97

GUEST CAST

HAROLD SPULLER
    Steven M. Porter
CHUCK FORSCH
    Sydney Lassick
ANGELO PINTERO
    Alex Bruhanski
DETECTIVE HUDAK
    Daniel Kamin
SERGEANT CONNEFF
    Gerry Naim
UNIFORMED OFFICER
    Ken Tremblett
MARTIN ALPERT
    Mike Puttonen
NURSE INNES
    Nancy Fish
KAREN KOSSEFF
    Chistine Willes
THE ATTORNEY
    Lorena Gale

DEATH TOLL

4 WOMEN: all with their throats cut
2 MEN: apnea of unknown cause,
    heart failure (natural causes)

seemed to ask why the Garrow-Ghast herself might use her death, the ultimate in retirement schemes, to pester a poor family of farmers. No one even questioned that she existed, though nowhere in the story does anyone see anything other than the spirits of those threatened! Despite her consistent absence from the scene, the locals who kept the story alive insisted on the ghost's existence. They even gave this faceless, formless entity a gender – they made it female!

In "Elegy," Shiban's spirits appeared to those about to die. So did the Garrow-Ghast, but, unlike Shiban's ghosts, it's difficult to determine if the Garrow-Ghast herself had a hand in the deaths of four members of the Darrow family, if it was the ultimate coincidence, or if she appeared to them *because* they were about to die. In Shiban's tale, the opposite is true, we're told *why* the ghosts appeared to Spuller and Scully in particular, but not why they appeared in the first place! Certainly not to be saved. Nor to say good-bye to someone particularly close to them. Not even to point the blame to their accusor!

Perhaps, like the Garrow-Ghast's audience, the X-Philes aren't meant to know everything about the working on "the other side"?

CODE NAME:

"Demons"

Case: XF-4X23-05-11-97

CASE SUMMARY

Special Agent Fox Mulder is having a bad day. When he's awakened by strangely familiar nightmares in a completely unfamiliar motel room, covered in the blood of two apparent murder victims, with the victims' car in his parking space and two bullets missing from his sidearm, even he's ready to admit things aren't looking good. Things look even worse when he realizes he's lost time once again – three days' worth! – and there isn't an alien in sight. Or is there?

CASE HISTORY
I Need That Like . . . A Hole In The Head?

Trephination, for most of us, is a nifty oddity that we first ran into in psych class or that really gory *National Geographic* issue that was otherwise notable only for its lack of naked pygmy women, which accounted for its being left in the library in the first place. It's not like ear- or nose-piercing, something teens goad one another into doing as a lark, and it certainly isn't the sort of treatment discussed daily in general practitioners' offices. While it remains a treatment of last resort for conditions like depressed skull fractures, with a few rare – not to mention colorful – exceptions trephination, the "art" of jabbing a hole through your skull, is pretty much a thing of the past. Oddly, from the literature available, it seems that trephination was first noticeable not for the hole it left in the patient's head but for the piece of skull that used to be there. One anthropologist wrote about a series of strange decorative pieces he'd discovered at a variety of sites: "It is difficult to avoid wondering if these tribes, like certain ones in Papua, are not headhunters. Disturbing as the thought may be, especially in a group we'd, perhaps romantically, considered progressive for their time, it is difficult to avoid as we continue to turn up amulets derived from what were surely human skulls. The pieces, varying only slightly in size from a square of perhaps

three-quarters of an inch per side, feature rough striations along each edge consistent with a number of the chipping-style implements indigenous to the region. A small hole, drilled most precisely in the centre of the 'amulet,' appears to have been made to accept a string or thong. Indeed, one example, discovered by Dr. Scoplin, was still attached to the remains of a thong of worked leather. The amulets themselves are further decorated, some with dyes, some with an ash mixture rubbed into carvings which were presumably completed after removal from the victim's skull." Similar "amulets" would turn up at dig sites as distant from each other as Peru and Turkey.

When trephinated skulls, complete with sizeable holes, were discovered in Europe, they were frequently taken to be battle injuries from an as yet undetermined weapon. The notion that the missing sections were trophies of one sort of another was toyed with from time to time, but, in Europe, war tended to be a hack-and-slash affair with little of the ritual common to South American or South Seas groups. That an enemy would take the time to neatly chisel his way through his victim's skull after beating him savagely just minutes before remained a contradictory, but tacitly accepted, idea even after the notion that Europeans had independently created the same nifty new weapon that was trephinating people half a world away was finally dropped.

Soon, in-depth attention turned from the cranial chips on their lengths of string to the skulls themselves, and an amazingly obvious, if completely overlooked, fact turned up. A significant number of skulls proved the "victims" had survived the procedure! A whole new avenue of inquiry quickly opened. If many of those who'd undergone the trephination procedure had not only survived, but – if the regeneration of bone was any indicator – flourished after the highly invasive procedure, wasn't it possible that what had been assumed to

Trivia Buster

23

THESE ARE THE EASY ONES! TAKE A SINGLE POINT FOR EACH CORRECT ANSWER.

1. Which unit of Hansen's Motel did Mulder wake up in?

2. How many rounds were missing from Mulder's gun?

3. What was written on the keyring Mulder found in his room?

4. To what famous case does Mulder compare his predicament?

5. For what magazine was Amy Cassandra a cover girl?

THESE WILL MAKE YOU THINK, SO GIVE YOURSELF TWO POINTS FOR A CORRECT RESPONSE.

6. What was Amy Cassandra's middle name?

7. What did the suicidal officer do to his photos?

8. From what illness did Scully think Amy Cassandra suffered?

9. Who was Amy Cassandra's psychologist?

10. Name the officer who shot himself.

Trivia Buster

23

<u>ONE POINTERS:</u>

1. 6.

2. 2.

3. "AMY."

4. The OJ Simpson trial.

5. Abductee.

<u>TWO POINTERS:</u>

6. Anne.

7. He cut himself out of them.

8. Waxman–Geschwind syndrome.

9. Dr. Charles Goldstein.

10. Michael Fazekas.

YOUR SCORE _____

be a war ritual was actually a medical treatment? Why else would anyone allow their neighbor to put a chisel to their head and whack away at will?

To find the answer to what conditions might have prompted early men to such drastic action, anthropologists turned to examples from modern history.

Modern "cutting-edge" (no pun intended) procedures of our time that might be considered equivalent included the drilling of burr holes to relieve subdural pressure, the removal of cranial sections to access interior tissue for surgical procedures, and the removal of injured sections of the cranium (i.e. depressed skull fractures) to prevent further injury to underlying tissues. Despite significant differences, or assumed differences, in the medical settings which accommodated patients from modern and pre-history, the end result was remarkably similar. Still, the notion that ancient medical men were diagnosing and treating brain injuries with reasonably high rates of success (once again judging from the ratio of skulls showing bone regrowth) was hard for many academics to swallow.

The research took a diametrically opposing viewpoint when anthropologists and archaeologists began, literally, tripping over trephinated skulls in Peru. In total, some 10,000 skulls sporting the now-familiar holes were uncovered. Even in modern times, in the largest population groupings, it would be unlikely for one in every ten individuals to have had someone poke holes in their skulls for any sound medical reason.

Thus was born the belief that not only physical ailment but psychological illness might well have been treated this way. In the void of any real information about ancient psychotherapy, it was easy for tales of witch-doctors releasing "demons" of one sort and another through holes in their patients' heads to flourish. The amulets that had been considered war trophies, and which had never fit particularly well into the medical model (unless you, too, have an Uncle Ernie who likes to display his gallstone on the fireplace mantel), became symbolic of the so-called spirits and evil humors that trephination came to be associated with.

In a sort of "reverse history" lesson, a whole model of myths, legends and medical treatments was created for the Mesoamericans, based more on the "romanticism" mentioned by that earlier anthropologist than on any tangible physical evidence from the skulls, the cranial pieces, or the sites where they were found.

In 1962, a Peruvian doctor, using precisely the tools identified as prehistorical trephination instruments, took drastic measures to intervene in a drastic situation involving a patient with severe head trauma. The tools were easily as effective as those in current medical use and the patient, who survived and was released just days later, had every reason to agree. That incident turned the attention of many in the field back to a medical survey of those skulls down in Peru. This time, a fairly detailed catalogue was made of a thousand of them, a good representative sample. Several factors came to light. One researcher, personally responsible for the cataloguing of four hundred and fifty skulls, determined that some two hundred and eighty "patients" had recovered and lived an average of eight to twelve years after the surgery. With an expected lifespan of just over thirty, that's not bad. A second researcher, working at a different site, where there were a number of bodies associated with the skulls, began a holistic study of the bodies, not just the heads. Though she was working with a smaller selection of skulls, a certain pattern of injuries – other than the obvious hole in the head – started to become apparent, a pattern similar to that found in modern-day epileptics! Just as there is a modern-day pattern of increased incidences of epilepsy in portions of the Chinese population, in comparison with worldwide figures, modern citizens of Peru also

How many secrets does
this woman carry?

suffer from that particular disease in higher than average numbers. In fact, that correlation is one of many items that indicate the land-bridge theory between Siberia and Alaska may well account for human beings living in the Americas at all! If prehistorical Peruvians, a large but tightly knit population, reflected a similar set of statistics, then the possibility of medical trephination on a wide scale begins to make sense once again.

Modern epilepsy treatment relies heavily on drug therapies, but at one point a surgical procedure which separated the hemispheres of the brain was one treatment being heavily studied and endorsed by the medical profession. Separating the hemispheres of the brain, for some patients, provided instant relief. Of course, that's still a pretty drastic form of treatment, with a host of unwanted side-effects, and in keeping with the less invasive philosophy being widely supported in all health fields drug therapies became better investigated and more effective, making dangerous surgeries less and less common.

In early Peruvian society, however, two things could have

contributed to a long-term preference for the surgical option. First of all, unlike many European societies, Peru was home to several anesthetic-producing plants. These plants, which even without fancy laboratories gave up not only local-type anesthetics but distillations capable of rendering people unconscious in a reliable way, made the trephination operation considerably less horrendous for an early Peruvian than his European cousin. The fact that the other locales where trephined skulls were located in large numbers, like Turkey and Southeast Asia, all produced plants with similar properties, suggests that the available pharmacopoeia might well have contributed to the number of patients willing to undergo surgery. The second reason is also plant-related. Although Peru had vast resources of anesthetics, it had few of the plants which would become common in the treatment of "falling sickness" elsewhere. Mongolia, with its relatively high incidence of epilepsy, produced no fewer than ten plants which were believed to be beneficial in its treatment. Chinese physicians had dozens of recipes based on the local flora. Peru had none. Neither did Turkey, Mexico or the South Sea islands, where trephined skulls regularly turn up.

The epilepsy–trephination connection, while intriguing from an anthropological and medical viewpoint, remains to be conclusively proven however, and in the absence of such definitive proof the colorful, often haunting, tales of demons being released from the heads of possessed individuals are certainly likely to stick in the average person's romantic mind.

It's romanticism of another sort altogether, though, that brought trephination back into general public awareness during the 1960s and 1970s. According to subculture lore, trephination has another, wholly unmedical, facet waiting for those brave enough to visit their local home improvement shop and pick up a common drill with a bit of oomph to its motor. If the news items that popped up in Denmark and

X Scully made excellent time getting to her partner! After answering his initial call for help at 4:50 a.m., she swung into the parking lot in front of his motel, a place she'd never been to before, in Providence, Rhode Island, at 6:15 a.m. Of course, she did leave a man in an unknown mental state without medical attention for those same 85 minutes!

Great Britain during that time are to be believed, at least half a dozen individuals either jointly or as soloists decided to give Do-It-Yourself trephination a try! Some cases, like that of Amedia Martin, who suffered from a variety of mental illness which convinced her something very close to the "demons" attributed to the Mesoamericans lived in her brain and were telling her to do terrible things, could be written off as mental aberrations, but some of these home surgeries were performed by people whom the medical profession would call perfectly sane! While the rest of their generation sought peace, love and sexual freedom, helping it along with a hefty dose of mind-altering chemicals, a small nook in the peace-love-rock-'n'-roll world was looking for its own version of Nirvana, the perfect, permanent high. Sometime during that period the brain–blood-volume theory gained limited fame. It postulated that when human beings took to walking upright, they lost some of their brains' bloodflow. In children, whose skull sutures (the "joints" in the cranium) have yet to completely fuse, the volume of blood reaching the brain is thought to be high; adults, with their fixed bones, are believed by some to suffer from a further blood-volume loss. To those seeking to regain the innocence, the enthusiasm, the seemingly unlimited learning potential, and the uninhibited outlook of a child, the answer seemed impossibly easy – just open up those sutures! The only problem is, of course, that removing the calcium and bone cells that form between the plates making up the cranium is completely impossible.

Undaunted, a very few seekers of renewed childhood reportedly decided to create their own "soft spot" by reviving the ancient art of trephination. The survivors became sort of retrograde icons who even set up their own travelling tent shows preaching the wonders of trephination. Lots of people seem to have listened, but the actual number of disciples were, perhaps not surprisingly, few. Body-piercing, tattooing, even branding have all remained as symbols of both rebellion and individuality, but it's doubtful that Black and Decker stock is about to surge on the basis of the revival of D-I-Y trephination.

CASE NOTES
Back From The Dead

Mulder's little Ketamine-assisted jaunt into his past puts him into a group even more exclusive than alien abduction victims. As Scully points out, in most of the world Ketamine and its variants are veterinary drugs, deemed more or less unsuited to human consumption. Why? Not because of any memory-enhancing ability the drug may or may not have, but because, for those who've experienced its "anesthetic" qualities, it's like a preview of death. Present-day Russia is one of the rare spots where Ketamine has a human use. There it's used as part of a regime to help cope with the exploding number of alcoholics that seem as much a side-effect of capitalism as the falling value of the rouble. When drug therapy, behavior-adjustment therapies, psychotherapy and everything else imaginable has failed, Ketamine becomes the chemical therapy of choice. One patient describes his results:

"First my lips, then the tips of my fingers, my feet, even the top of my head, all went numb. It was like freezing to death in cold water, the chill ate inwards, towards my heart. The lids of my eyes no longer moved when I wanted them to, I couldn't feel any part of my body except the slowing beat of my heart. I heard my breath whistling through my throat, heard the thudding of my pulse just below my ear, then nothing!

"I couldn't hear, I couldn't speak, I couldn't even see. My eyes were open, but I couldn't focus on anything. Then it got dark. I died. I know I did. The doctors say I didn't, but I did. That is why I am so happy now, why I will never drink again. I don't want to die. Not like that. Not aware of every beat of my heart – even the last."

CASE CREDITS

WRITTEN BY:R. W. Goodwin
DIRECTED BY: Kim Manners
ORIGINAL PRODUCTION
    NUMBER: 4X23
ORIGINAL US AIRDATE: 05/11/97

GUEST CAST

YOUNG SAMANTHA
    Vanessa Morley
YOUNG MRS. MULDER
    Shelley Adam
YOUNG BILL MULDER
    Dean Aylesworth
YOUNG FOX MULDER
    Alex Haythorne
YOUNG CIGARETTE-SMOKING MAN
    Chris Owens
IMHOF
    Terry Jang Barclay
HOUSEKEEPER
    Rebecca Harker
MEDICAL EXAMINER
    Andrew Johnston
DR. CHARLES GOLDSTEIN
    Mike Nussbaum
DET. JOE CURTIS
    Jay Acovone
ADMITTING OFFICER
    Eric Breker

DEATH TOLL

2 MEN: 1 shot to death, 1 committed
    suicide.
1 WOMAN: committed suicide

Other patients remark on the drug's amazing capacity to dissociate mind from body.

"You know you're dying. There's no question in your mind. But you don't care."

"It was the first time in years I hadn't felt that demon, the drink, clawing at my mind. I knew my mind could exist without the booze. When I came back from wherever it is you go, I could almost remember what it felt like to be dead, to know the body is a conquerable thing. I just don't need to drink to achieve that."

Still, for all the apparent effectiveness of the drug, and despite the relief many alcoholics seem to find in the Death and Re-Birth treatments, few of them come back for a second dosing.

"No. Never again. I'd rather not drink than go through that again, and the not drinking is hard enough."

CODE NAME:

"Gethsemane"

Case: XF-4X24-05-18-97

CASE SUMMARY

The discovery of an "alien," perfectly preserved, in an ice cave high in the Canadian Arctic soon has Mulder hiking up the side of the St. Elias Mountains with an anthropologist already tied to at least one hoax. Scully, refusing to accompany him, remains in Washington, tackling the physical evidence contained in ice core samples from the same site. Violence follows them both and, in the final analysis, Scully appears before the man who originally assigned her to the X-Files to condemn all of Mulder's four years of investigation.

CASE HISTORY
A History of Hoaxes

"The Piltdown Man hoax wasn't uncovered for forty years – until it failed a carbon-dating test. And that wasn't even very good!"
– SPECIAL AGENT FOX MULDER, *on hoaxes*

No student of history, no scientist, no seeker of the truth can exist in the 1990s without acknowledging the possibility of deliberate deception, sloppy science and haphazard hoaxes. Cold fusion, crop circles and even Mendel's infamous pea plant results have suffered from close inspection. When Piltdown Man's "discovery" was announced in 1913, the world – and its scientists – were a considerably more naive, more incredulous, lot. Not that there hadn't been hoaxes before – far from it. Nor were the hoaxes obscure little events easily overlooked by the scientific community.

The experience of Dr. Bartholomew Adam Beringer, who practised his palaeontology almost before the field had a name, is a case in point. Amazing as it seems to us, early fossil-diggers weren't exactly sure what fossils were. Sure, a few, a very few, rock impressions bore a vague resemblance to living creatures, but, the vast majority appeared completely outlandish to early 18th century scientists. Small wonder then that, with science failing to provide an explanation, the other major force of the day, religion, would step in to fill the void.

EYEWITNESS STATEMENT

"The lies are so deep, the only way to cover them is to create something even more incredible. They invented *you*. Your regression hypnosis, the story of your sister's abduction, the lies they told your father... You wanted to believe so badly."

Michael Kritschgau,

US Army Research Division

For his time, Beringer's theory, that fossils were simply God's playthings, objects created for his personal pleasure, maybe moulds for creatures yet to be, or for God's discards, wasn't all that unreasonable. In fact, Beringer was a well-travelled and well-received speaker. So well-received that, according to some of his colleagues, he also became a bit big for his britches.

Two men, Ignatz Roderick and George von Eckart, decided to prick his bubble.

First, they planted fake fossils in Beringer's favorite dig site. Neither Beringer nor his colleagues clued in.

It wasn't long before Roderick and von Eckart were back at the site again. This time, they sowed truly outrageous fakes. Suns, moons, and outright art decorated this batch. To their utter amazement, only a handful of people questioned the new finds! For Beringer, here was proof of God's hand at work! When Beringer's frantic digging turned up rocks with Greek, Latin and Hebrew phrases, all of which translated to "God," carved into them, Beringer published his own book – despite the growing number of people who were now pointing out the obvious chisel marks on the stones, and the fact that the more Beringer dug, the more exotic his finds became.

When Beringer's theories had been committed to paper, and Beringer himself had invested a considerable amount of his reputation, as well as his money, in the volume, Roderick and von Eckart decided they'd found the perfect opportunity to expose Beringer's gullibility. Beringer, however, responded in a way neither Roderick nor von Eckart could have possibly predicted, though it would become a standard counter-argument for dozens of hoaxes to come.

Instead of being horrified at the deception, Beringer promptly accused Roderick and von Eckart of plotting to undermine him, of planting their fakes in an attempt to cast doubt on God's genuine work! Thereafter ensued a series of accusations and counter-accusations that would have done almost any ufologist proud. Not too surprisingly, all three men

24

Answers

KEEP TRACK OF YOUR TOTAL SCORE. SEE WHERE YOU'D END UP IN THE X-FILEAN WORLD OF HIERARCHIES, SHADOW GOVERNMENTS, AND CONSPIRACIES.

ONE POINTERS:

1. Carbon-dating.

2. Under his tent.

3. A chainsaw.

4. The Smithsonian.

5. Faith.

TWO POINTERS:

6. Section Chief Scott Blevins.

7. St. Elias Mountains, Yukon Territory, Canada.

8. According to his ice core calculations, 200 years.

9. The Paleoclimatology Lab at American University.

10. For the United States Army, in their Research Division, at the Pentagon.

YOUR SCORE _____

soon found it difficult to generate any support from serious scientists.

A century later, another generation of hoaxers was at work in North America where George Hull was busy preparing his own assault on science, religion, and the gullible public. With the assistance of a pair of sculptors from Chicago, Hull swiftly obtained the "Cardiff Giant" which would soon be "discovered" on the farm of a William Newell who had directed his workmen to start a well in a most particular spot. Within weeks, it was being heralded as a petrified man, an example of the Biblical giants his theologian-friend insisted were historic figures as well as biblical symbols. Though the Giant was originally intended solely as the means to win his bet with the theologian, Hull was quick to recognize the statue's effect on those who saw it.

So was P.T. Barnum. He offered Hull the exorbitant sum of $60,000 for it!

Hoping to hang onto his statue and make that much or more himself, Hull displayed the statue on the site. Unfortunately, Hull wasn't the showman Barnum was, and Barnum simply created a duplicate for his own display, which further reduced the amount Hull could hope to realize.

In any case, it wasn't long before the sculptors owned up to their part in the fraud, as did Hull, but that didn't stop the "Cardiff Giant" from being included in dozens of articles who would claim it proved the Bible was a piece of authentic history instead of an amalgamation of history and teaching-tales, a view that would later become more widely accepted. Even after Hull and Co. admitted their parts in the hoax, such luminaries of the time as Oliver Wendell Holmes and Ralph Waldo Emerson, men whose work was widely available, continued to extol its antiquity.

As the Leakeys, who would later discover the authentic remains of a significant human skeleton they dubbed "Lucy," would later note, "It sometimes seems that the lay public is primed to accept the outlandish before the more common-place, but equally amazing, truths become known."

While both the Cardiff Giant and Beringer's Rocks hoaxes were perpetrated when scientists were pretty much limited to a magnifying glass and their common sense to develop complex theories, technology and the spread of scientific methodology certainly haven't eliminated hoaxing. George Jammal, an Israeli actor who had some spare time between jobs, pulled a hoax as recently as 1992 that would have done old P.T. Barnum proud.

It all began when Jammal picked up a scrap of wood from an abandoned railway tie, took it home with him, and baked it in the oven. Things escalated quickly when he claimed to be an amateur archaeologist who discovered this fragment atop Mount Ararat, a location previously suggested as the resting place of Noah's Ark. A production company called Sun was soon filming a documentary "The Amazing Discovery of Noah's Ark," which aired amid considerable hype on CBS.

Despite the prompt criticism of dozens of qualified scientists, and their numerous requests for standard testing of this "ark fragment," neither Jammal nor his piece of wood were forced to defend themselves. Sun, who had two more specials in the works for CBS, "Revelations" and "The UFO Phenomena," leaped to Jammal's defence, quickly followed by CBS. It seems likely that both companies would have continued supporting the bogus claims, and ensuring the faked evidence was kept out of the hands of any legitimate scientists, if not for one extraordinary turn of affairs. Jammal went national to inform the world that he'd done it, he'd committed a hoax, a hoax that might have gone on indefinitely, a hoax that neither CBS nor Sun had questioned at any point during the filming or airing of their "investigative documentary." It was Jammal who pointed out again and again just how slipshod the reporting had been. Even his most basic claim, that he'd been to Mount Ararat, well inside Turkey, was never checked. Jammal not only was never asked to support his claims of having found the ark, he wasn't even asked to present a passport or other proof of ever being where he claimed to have found a huge boat atop a mountain.

Jammal's success in a supposedly technologically advanced, and cynical, age doesn't explain how a hoax like Piltdown Man might pass muster, but it should underscore how much less was known of palaeontology and the authentication of artifacts back in 1912 when Charles Dawson, an amateur archaeologist, first announced to the world that man's "missing link" with his simian ancestors had been unearthed in a gravel quarry in Sussex, England. Piltdown Man, as the scraps of skull and jaw fragments Dawson presented would come to be known, was in many ways a hoax waiting to happen.

P.T. Barnum once said that there's no man easier to fool than one "with expectations." In many ways, it was Barnum's business motto. From the Fejee Mermaid to Jo-Jo, the dog-faced boy, Barnum made a fortune giving people the things they suspected just might exist. Piltdown Man was a hoax whose time had come.

Darwin's "The Origin of Species" was still shaking the religious and scientific community.

Neanderthal man had been discovered in 1856 and important examples would continue to appear across Europe, especially in Germany – but not in Great Britain.

Does it seem like it's been a long time since Scully and Mulder looked up at anything in silent wonder?

Cro-Magnon, the next major discovery, turned up just across the channel in France, Britain's long-time nemesis, in 1868 and still there was no sign of anything important in England. Peking Man and its associated artifacts began pointing to even more ancient origins for man, but still there was no sign of the Missing Link, no way to connect these pre-hominids with modern man. Yet it was a group of British scientists who were the strongest proponents of the theory that man and apes had common ancestors. Without physical evidence, their theory, intriguing as it was, couldn't withstand serious scientific inquiry. There was simply no proof and, while that was a situation that a fictional Mulder might almost come to terms with, it was a galling day-to-day reality for many of Britain's scientific community.

So, when Dawson suddenly appeared with a specimen exhibiting an apparently human, if thickened, skull and an ape-like jaw with humanoid teeth, his specimen couldn't help but fulfill not only a scientific likelihood, but the ardent wishes of more than one patriotic Englishman. Though nationalistic feeling, like primitive technology, is no excuse for a hoax to survive for forty years, it's undoubtedly a factor in what would become one of science's own most intriguing mysteries because, even today, with all the technology available to historical detectives, it's entirely possible that such vague motives may present the pivotal clue to finally discovering just who planted Piltdown Man.

Everyone knows why Roderick and von Eckart set up their colleague Beringer – they couldn't stand him! Their motive was simply to make a public fool of someone who rubbed them the wrong way with his close-minded insistence that only he could possibly explain the existence of fossils.

Likewise, Hull's motivation for creating the Cardiff Giant is well-documented. He'd made a bet and he intended to win it. The rest was simple greed.

Even Jammal had a reason for stepping forward when he

X BLOOPER! Oops, somebody botched the research on this one. It wasn't carbon-14 dating that proved Piltdown Man was a forgery. It was fluorine testing, something that Mulder should have known since carbon-14 testing didn't become widespread until after 1953 when Piltdown had already been acknowledged a forgery.

X CATCH IT? The usual "THE TRUTH IS OUT THERE" section of the credits was replaced for this episode with "BELIEVE THE LIE."

did. He could have exposed the ludicrous "investigation" of his Noah's Ark find at any time. Instead, he kept quiet until he realized that CBS fully intended to continue with its sensational, poorly researched, series of specials. He'd imagined that, in the wake of scientific criticism accompanying "The Discovery of Noah's Ark," CBS would abandon those plans. When they didn't, he took the next, to him, logical step.

In each of those hoaxes, some motive became evident fairly quickly, but Piltdown Man was different. No one ever claimed responsibility. Not that there was a lack of suspects, but, as Mulder puts it to Kritschgau nearly a century later, "Why?" Why would anyone invest nearly a decade, or in the case of UFO reports, half a century, "inventing" a hoax? Where's the motive?

In the case of Piltdown Man, motives abounded.

The first to come under scrutiny, of course, was Charles Dawson himself. He'd found the damn thing, not to mention a second dual-trait skull when it was suggested that the pieces of Piltdown Man (I) might have been from two separate creatures. The physical area under study was large. That one man would find two such specimens seems incredible to his detractors, solid proof to his supporters. That Dawson was an ambitious man who, like Arlinsky in "Gethsemane," had already been tied to several possible deceptions, even if he was merely one of many gullible victims and not a ringleader, didn't make his find any more reliable to many of his colleagues. Nor did contradictory stories about when and where the fragments were actually found make his case stronger. Even if Dawson didn't act alone to perpetrate the hoax, any number of co-conspirators, all with their own motives, were available.

Dawson wasn't the only one present on each of the significant discoveries. A man named Hargreaves, the actual digger hired by Dawson, *was* there from the beginning. He knew when and where Dawson was likely to dig. Many have suggested it would have been impossible for anyone to have pulled it all off without his co-operation. If not for Dawson, well, then for someone else, someone whose motive was equally strong.

Grafton Elliot Smith became a member of the team early, but, unlike Dawson, was an expert in a number of the fields that would have been required to perpetrate so technical a scheme. He was an anatomist of considerable skill, certainly more than enough to quickly identify the fact that the skull and jaw that Dawson had claimed fit together, in fact had no physical point of connection! He also conveniently missed the fact that the teeth associated with the finds didn't quite match either and the fact that he wasn't physically present for key events is meaningless if one assumes a conspiracy. His motive? The prestige of being part of an important find.

The third member of the team, Woodward, though seldom mentioned as either the original hoaxer or an accomplice, had equally powerful motives. At the time of the "finds," Woodward was involved in an active campaign to become the next Director of the British Museum of Natural History, a plum assignment. With Piltdown Man confirming the very hypothesis that Woodward was busy advocating, Woodward became very fashionable very fast. Once installed in his new position, he also became the official custodian of the Piltdown Man artifacts – a fact Mulder would certainly find suspicious. As Mulder told Arlinsky, it's rather difficult to authenticate or disprove

Since the bad days of Deep Throat, Mulder's "contacts" have become progressively more suspect, perhaps more suspect than many of the "bad guys" he chases.

CASE CREDITS

WRITTEN BY: Chris Carter
DIRECTED BY: R.W. Goodwin
ORIGINAL PRODUCTION
   NUMBER: 4X24
ORIGINAL US AIRDATE: 05/18/97

GUEST CAST

SECTION CHIEF SCOTT BLEVINS
   Charles Cioffi
AGENT HEDIN
   Nancy Kerr
DET. REMPULSKI
   Bob Freeman
MRS. SCULLY
   Sheila Larkin
BILL SCULLY, JR.
   Pat Skipper
FATHER MCCUE
   Arnie Walters
MICHAEL KRITSCHGAU
   John Finn
ARLINSKY
   Matthew Walker
BABCOCK
   James Sutorius
ROLSTON
   John Oliver
OSTELHOFF
   Steve Makaj
DR. VITAGLIANO
   Barry W. Levy

DEATH TOLL

6 MEN: shot to death

anything when the same people judging the evidence are also the opposition. It's also rather difficult for most objective observers to "forget" that many of the bones seen with the Piltdown artifacts, to provide the Piltdown Man with the impression of antiquity by association, weren't exactly common, everyday sorts of bones. Some were incredibly rare. Yet, of all those involved, it was Woodward who was the most capable of obtaining them. Once installed at the British Museum of Natural History, he had access to an even greater range of artifacts just at the time when even more unusual items were appearing at Piltdown. For many scientists, both then and now, the provenance of the bones found can't do anything but implicate Woodward.

Almost everyone to set foot on the site has come under suspicion. Even Sir Arthur Conan Doyle has been targeted. His motive? Like his most famous creation, Sherlock Holmes, Doyle loved a puzzle. He was also a zealous mystic and a spiritualist who became disenchanted with the scientific community after they trashed the reputation of one of his long-time friends. If that hardly seems enough to cast suspicion on him, those who believe in his guilt point out that Doyle lived just a few miles from Piltdown, had visited the site, was an amateur fossil-hunter in his own right and, to top it off, he wrote a book, *The Lost World*, about dinosaurs and humans that some say gives out dozens of clues about Piltdown Man. Of course, there are also those like Charles Manson who found the instructions to begin a race war within the innocent verses of some Beatles tunes . . .

Most recently, another man, who seemed to have been only superficially involved in the dig, has been almost universally acclaimed as the one and only Piltdown hoaxer. Up until 1996, those curious about the Piltdown Man hoax faced the same basic problem Mulder has for the past four years, tons of theories, plenty of motive, but absolutely no hard proof. Then, while clearing out a section of the Museum, a strange collection of bones turned up. Just like the Piltdown Man bones which were now known to be a hoax, these bones were tinted with a specific recipe of elements. Just like the Piltdown Man site, an amazing range of bones types were represented. And whose initials were on the trunk? None other than Martin A. C. Hinton, a curator at the Museum during the discoveries at Piltdown. Following up on that clue, investigators turned to Hinton's estate and discovered, among his many effects, a collection of teeth in vials. All the teeth had been treated to look old – just like the ones at Piltdown. All the teeth had been filed in a particular style – just like the ones at Piltdown. And, just like everyone associated with the hoax, Hinton had powerful motives based in the unbelievably vicious circle of scientists working at the Museum – or hoping to work there. Among his other complaints against those at Piltdown was the fact that Hinton had been refused a coveted position at the prestigious institution.

Still, even with the so-called "smoking gun," there's still no absolute proof against even Hinton! The "Incredible Randi" spends a considerable percentage of his time creating hoaxes, not to perpetrate on an unsuspecting public, but to expose those who would. Hinton, despite being shunted off into a scientific backwater away from his own field, was still an expert on fossils. Given the right circumstances, a case could be made that Hinton was doing what any good scientist would do when faced with a puzzle, try to replicate the so-called "evidence," then expose the procedure. After all this time, it's tough to determine which came first, Hinton's experiments or Piltdown Man.

The inclusion of the Piltdown Man hoax in "Gethsemane" rings true on a number of levels. "Truth" is a notoriously elusive thing. Whether it's UFOs or Missing Links, the lessons learned from the Piltdown Hoax remain as relevant to modern scientists – and ufologists – as they should have been to the team who started digging up bones at Piltdown.

TRIVIA BUSTER SCORECARD

All right! The end is in sight. Tally up those numbers and see where you fall in the hierarchy of shadow-seekers and conspiracy buffs! And, remember, someone is always watching – no cheating! (Unless, of course, you can cheat and still retain "plausible deniability.")

1–25: There is no polite way to say this – you're a bigger "doofus" than Pendrell! Even he could figure out who the competition was! Get thee to the nearest video rental shop, or raid the rather ragged tape collections of real X-Philes, and try not to fall asleep before they flash "THE TRUTH IS OUT THERE."

26–100: OK, there probably are jobs for people like you within the Bureau. We hear Holly needs someone to help her arrange her paperclips, but, frankly, even she's not that desperate!

101–150: Hey, we might have just the job for you. As the old adage goes, "Those who can do, those who can't teach, and those who can't do either, well, they administrate." May I introduce you to Section Head Blevins?

151–200: OK, you've made it into the Bureau and have become part of the first line of defence – what do you mean, cannon fodder?! Has someone been using that Ruby Ridge film in the training rooms again?

201–225: We want you. We need you. And we just happen to have an opening that came up . . . unexpectedly. You've never heard of an Agent Mulder, have you?

226–?: Yes, we realize you wanted a posting in the Washington Bureau offices, but have you ever been to New York City? My colleagues and I have an opening there, not to mention a wonderful, old-fashioned sort of club that's right across from the UN.

ABOUT THE AUTHOR

N.E. Genge lives and works out of the far reaches of northern Canada. She is a documentary scriptwriter as well as the author of two historical biographies. Her fiction has appeared in *Aboriginal Science Fiction, Asimov's Science Fiction* and *Story*. As the author of *The Unofficial X-Files Companion, The New Unofficial X-Files Companion, The Lexicon* and *Millennium: The Unofficial Companion Volume One and Volume Two*, she is something of an expert on Chris Carter's creations.